EFFECTIVE CHRISTIAN LEADERS IN THE GLOBAL WORKPLACE

EFFECTIVE CHRISTIAN LEADERS IN THE GLOBAL WORKPLACE

PETER SHAW

Paternoster:
thinking faith

Paternoster Publishing
A Ministry of Biblica
We welcome your questions and comments.

USA   1820 Jet Stream Drive, Colorado Springs, CO 80921 www.authenticbooks.com
India   Logos Bhavan, Medchal Road, Jeedimetla Village, Secunderabad 500 055, A.P.

Effective Christian Leaders in the Global Workplace
ISBN-13: 978-1-93406-884-7

A catalog record for this book is available through the Library of Congress.

Printed in the United States of America

Dedicated to Nick and Hazel Whitehead,
who have been a source of encouragement and challenge
to many who are growing into leadership roles

CONTENTS

ACKNOWLEDGMENTS

As I look back, there have been many formative influences on my journey that led to writing this book. In my early teens, two leaders of our youth group, Norman Anfield (a banker) and Jack Ripley (a corn merchant), brought a practical approach to living out one's faith in a busy world. At Durham University, Gerald Blake, one of my geography professors, inspired me to seek to interrelate my aspirations about faith and work.

A particularly formative year was 1970–71, the year I spent at Regent College in Vancouver as one of its first full-time students. Regent's vision was to develop leaders who could live out their Christian faith effectively in a wide range of jobs and professions. The injunction to "go out into the world" meant bringing the message and relevance of the Christian gospel into every area of life. Particular inspiration came from the founding principal of Regent College, Jim Houston, who encouraged me to be adventurous in thinking about both faith and work.

Throughout a varied career in UK government departments, I observed both politicians and officials who brought a Christian perspective to their leadership roles. Among politicians, Mark Carlisle, Alistair Burt, and Stephen Timms were a particular encouragement. Among officials, Philip Halsey, Roger Dawe, and Hugh Taylor always brought a thoughtful approach rooted in their Christian values. When I moved into coaching,

Robin Linnecar, my colleague, was an excellent mentor, enabling me to work through the interrelationships between faith, work, and coaching.

I talked to a wide range of people as I prepared this book. Their perspectives have been invaluable, and I am grateful to them all. I want to thank explicitly those individuals I quote extensively: Stephen Bampfylde, Matthew Frost, Matt Baggott, and Eddie Donaldson. I am thankful for their willingness to share their stories.

I am grateful to Hugh Taylor for writing the foreword to the book. Hugh has held a range of different leadership positions within the UK government. For the last few years he has held a most sensitive position as permanent secretary at the government's Department of Health. He has led the department skillfully as it has tackled an array of demanding issues. He has always brought practical wisdom and built trust with people from a broad spectrum of perspectives.

Lynda Donaldson and Ian Angell read the text in draft and provided very thoughtful comments. Jackie Tookey and Tracy Easthope typed the manuscript with skill and fortitude. Claire Pratt has arranged my schedule with care so that I was able to include discussions on this subject with a host of people. Helen Burtenshaw has provided much helpful advice during the final stages of completing the text.

I am thankful for Mark Finnie of Authentic UK, who believed the project was worth taking forward; for Volney James, who commissioned the book on behalf of Authentic; and for John Dunham and Andrew Sloan for their practical assistance in turning the manuscript into this book. Andrew has been a wise and thoughtful editor.

I am grateful to my wife, Frances, and our children, Graham, Ruth, and Colin, for their encouragement. They always seem to sense when they are answering a question that could lead to a story in a book!

This book is dedicated to Nick and Hazel Whitehead, who, in their different ways, have been a source of encouragement to a wide range of people developing their leadership capabilities. For Nick, this has been the case within both the parish where he is vicar and the wider area for which he is rural dean, as well as with students training for ministry. For Hazel, it has been through working with a cross section of students training for ministry or through providing professional development for those in different forms of Christian ministry.

In the same way that I have been encouraged by many people on my journey, I hope that this book will be a source of stimulus to Christians tackling different issues in a variety of different contexts, irrespective of age, denomination, or geography.

OTHER BOOKS BY PETER SHAW

Mirroring Jesus as Leader. Cambridge: Grove, 2004.

Conversation Matters: How to Engage Effectively with One Another. London: Continuum, 2005.

The Four Vs of Leadership: Vision, Values, Value-Added, Vitality. Chichester, UK: Capstone, 2006.

Finding Your Future: The Second Time Around. London: Darton, Longman and Todd, 2006.

Business Coaching: Achieving Practical Results through Effective Engagement (coauthored with Robin Linnecar). Chichester, UK: Capstone, 2007.

Making Difficult Decisions: How to Be Decisive and Get the Business Done. Chichester, UK: Capstone, 2008.

Riding the Rapids: How to Navigate through Turbulent Times (coauthored with Jane Stephens). London: Praesta, 2008.

Deciding Well: A Christian Perspective on Making Decisions as a Leader. Vancouver: Regent College Publishing, 2009.

Raise Your Game: How to Succeed at Work. Chichester, UK: Capstone, 2009.

FOREWORD

In the *Audacity of Hope* (p. 207), Barack Obama speaks about the importance to him of seeing and experiencing faith—and specifically the Christian faith—as an "active, palpable agent in the world." How Christians bring that insight to life in the world of work is the challenge that Peter Shaw prompts and then probes in this characteristically thought-provoking work.

If as Christians with leadership responsibilities at work we are not living out, experiencing, and drawing on our faith when we are at work, we are diminishing ourselves and, more importantly, the work of the Holy Spirit in what is necessarily a big part of our lives. That does not mean—for me anyway—that the work environment is to be abused as a pulpit. But nor is it a separate, sealed domain where only secular values apply and Christianity can be switched off. It is just where we ought to both "feel the difference" of being a Christian and, as Peter says, rise to the challenge of "making a difference": faith as an "active, palpable agent" in the world of work.

I have known Peter for many years as a colleague, as a friend, and now as a coach. He has worked in leadership roles of the highest levels of central government. As an experienced coach and facilitator he has worked closely with hundreds of people at all levels in the public, private, and voluntary sectors. He is a lay preacher and an established author. A strong vein of wisdom, warmth, and humor permeates all his relationships.

It is our good fortune that Peter has drawn on this deep well of experience and poured it into this book. It is a rich resource, for us to use as individuals or in groups, built around what it means for the Christian at work to be rooted, radical, reflective, and renewed.

The four Rs make a striking framework, and Peter works through this sensitively and searchingly. His approach is open and subtle. Anyone looking for dogmatism will be sent away empty-handed. As with any good coach, there are as many questions as answers. Much of what he says will come as reinforcement of principles and practice that may already be familiar. But as I read one of Peter's references to the scene in John's Gospel where Jesus washes the feet of his disciples—one that resonates with lessons for the Christian about leadership as service—I was reminded of a painting of that very scene that hangs in the Tate Gallery in London. The painting is a long-standing favorite of mine. What I have always loved about it is the expression the artist (Ford Brown) has captured on St. Peter's face as he looks down on Jesus in this memorable act of service. It is, above all, one of surprise.

Peter has served us through this book. Expect, then, as you read it, not only reinforcement but also, as I found in passage after passage, the jolt of surprise—and the learning that comes from it. You are in good hands.

Sir Hugh Taylor
Permanent Secretary, UK Department of Health

INTRODUCTION

We live in a rapidly changing world with huge uncertainties. We can feel battered by economic and political change. We live in a global workplace, thereby increasing the level of our uncertainty and anxiety. The future often seems unclear, and we can be struggling with a whole raft of work and personal dilemmas at the same time.

Often it feels as if we are seeing through a glass darkly, without the confidence we would ideally like to have. On other occasions we are inspired by our work and encouraged by those around us. We feel that we are making a difference, with others benefiting from our modest contribution. We go home at the end of the day with a spring in our step, delighted to have the opportunity to work with others and be part of a positive, supportive environment.

This book is written for those who have a Christian perspective and are either working in the secular world or supporting and encouraging those who are working in the secular world. The themes apply equally, whether work for you is in the public, private, or voluntary sector. I hope the themes will resonate whatever your denomination or tradition and whatever part of the world you live in, while recognizing that there will be important cultural differences.

Some of you will come from a background where a Christian perspective is important but where church attendance may not be part of your current lifestyle. Others of you will be very committed to your local church. For some there will be no opportunity to talk with friends about dilemmas you face at work; for others there will be regular opportunity to reflect with friends through prayer groups or Bible study groups.

We live in an age where there is both a growing interest and acceptance of spirituality as well as a political correctness, which means that expressing a particular faith perspective might be discouraged. The openness to spirituality does provide a context to talk about values and to question accepted perspectives. The emphasis on political correctness reinforces the importance of building relationships of mutual understanding and not forcing our views down people's throats.

The Christian is invited to live the gospel in every area of life: that is, within family, community, and career. A Christian perspective is not just for Sundays, nor is it about insisting dogmatically that you are right and forcing your views on others in the work environment.

This book is not full of easy answers, but I hope it provides prompts for thought, reflection, conversation, and prayer that will enable you to be more confident in your faith perspective and willing to contribute in new and different ways. Each section includes questions for reflection, which I hope will be useful for both individuals and groups. I encourage you to come on a journey with me through this book, listening to the views of a variety of different people and then crystallizing some of your own thoughts and next steps.

The journey we travel in the book takes us through four Rs: *rooted, radical, reflective,* and *renewed.*

- *Rooted*: Who and what are your beliefs, values, and actions rooted in?
- *Radical*: How best do you live and act at a time of economic and global change in a way that applies Christian principles at work and ensures that difficult decisions are made well?
- *Reflective*: How do you listen, learn, and keep nourished, retaining a good balance of life while coping effectively with failure and disappointment?

- *Renewed*: How do you ensure that you keep learning and thinking ahead about your contribution and the use of your gifts, time, and energy, with an openness to taking next steps according to the prompting of the Holy Spirit?

I am not arrogant enough to think that Christians come with a monopoly on wisdom, but they do come with a distinct perspective. As believers, we should have the confidence that our contribution can make a difference. William Wilberforce wrote of being "diligent in the business of life," and his persistence led to the abolition of the UK slave trade. His approach was rooted in Christian principles and full of determination, regardless of the discouragement he received along the way.

This book draws on the experience of a wide range of people from the public, private, and voluntary sectors, including chief executives, politicians, senior police leaders, international bankers, and senior government officials. I draw from my own experience as a director general in the UK government in my first career and coaching senior leaders, along with speaking and writing about leadership themes in a secular context, in my second career. When I am working in a secular context, I normally include spirituality themes in what I say or write without forcing it upon people. This leads to interesting and thoughtful discussions, with most people being open to reflecting holistically on their physical, intellectual, emotional, and spiritual well-being.

I believe the time is right to reflect on many of the issues in this book. I hope the result for you will be some prompts for reflection and some points of action.

One final thought: Don't read this book out of duty. As Christians, we are often in danger of doing things because we think we ought to. I encourage you to leave the sense of *ought* behind and to read through this book because you want to and because you have a sense of Christian vocation that you want to nurture and grow and be able to share in the workplace context. I encourage you, as you approach your work, to "sing for joy to God our strength" (Psalm 81:1).

Peter Shaw

Godalming, England

April 2009

ROOTED

This chapter looks at what our beliefs and actions are rooted in. It starts with God's created order, looks at Jesus as leader, considers living the Christian themes, and asks when toughness or forgiveness is the right Christian response. It reflects on embedding the fruit of the Spirit, understanding human nature, and growing in self-awareness. Being rooted is about being "as wise as serpents and as innocent as doves."

WHY IS IT IMPORTANT TO BE ROOTED?

Our views can oscillate widely. We are pushed by the views in the media in one direction on one day and then in a very different direction a few months later. If we move between different locations, we can feel rootless and unloved.

Being rooted is not about being stuck in one place with one set of views. It is not the staleness and boredom that come from sitting in our small corner and thinking that all the world around us is wrong. Being rooted is about knowing what matters to us—being clear about the cornerstones of our beliefs and values. It means recognizing the foundation stones of our lives while being open to developing understanding and wisdom. Being rooted is using our intellectual, emotional, spiritual, and physical awareness to the best possible effect.

The apostle Paul encouraged the Colossians to be rooted in Christ Jesus as Lord. He wrote: "So then, just as you received Christ Jesus as

Lord, continue to live your lives in him, rooted and built up in him, strengthened in the faith as you were taught, and overflowing with thankfulness" (Colossians 2:6–7).

GOD'S CREATED ORDER

Rodney Green has written an excellent book entitled *90,000 Hours: Managing the World of Work*. He starts with God's creativity as evidenced in the early chapters of Genesis. Green illustrates that as Genesis progresses God works to create light and darkness, sky, sea and fertile land, stars and planets, and creatures of water, air, and land, including human beings. In all this there is beauty, profusion, life, color, contrast, variety, and richness. At the same time, however, tension and disharmony lurk just below the surface of the action.

Green suggests that since God is our Creator, imitating his example should underpin our approach to life in his creation. In particular:

- God created human beings and put them "in the Garden of Eden to work it and take care of it" (Genesis 2:15).
- God made human beings in his image and gave them the opportunity to reflect his qualities as Creator and Redeemer in every part of their lives, including work.
- God delights to share in and support our creative cooperation with him in bringing order and meaning to his universe.[1]

As a biblical definition of work, Green suggests that it is "the daily exertion, paid or unpaid, in contrast to rest and leisure, which is consistent with God's will, image, and design."[2] He sees the qualities of God the Creator that are relevant to our work as rational, righteous, responsible, restful, and relational.

---

1.   Rodney Green, *90,000 Hours: Managing the World of Work* (Bletchley, UK: Scripture Union, 2002), 22.
2.   Ibid., 23.

- *Rational*: The central thrust of God's activity is to bring order and meaning to his creation and thereby sustain it.
- *Righteous*: He gives prominence to "whatever is true, whatever is noble, whatever is right, whatever is pure, whatever is lovely, whatever is admirable" (Philippians 4:8).
- *Responsible*: With the freedoms God gives us to develop and enjoy his creation, we are expected to take care of both it and ourselves (Genesis 2:15).
- *Restful*: Rhythm and rest accompany all God's activities; "and there was evening, and there was morning" is repeated throughout the creation account.
- *Relational*: He values the relationship he has with us, his creation, offering humankind his friendship.[3]

Green's conclusion is that since we are created in the image of God, our work expresses his creativity. Creativity should enliven everything it touches with deeper order, purpose, and meaning. He suggests,

> We need to look more closely at God's character to recover what it means to reflect his image, since we are called to do this in every aspect of our work. We could start by reviewing our attitudes to work in general, as well as our attitudes to our own contributions at work. He calls us to cooperate with him by bringing order, purpose and meaning to our small part of his enterprise. In doing so, our individual creativity, skills and interests will find expression alongside those of others.[4]

A key starting point is that it is our privilege, dignity, and responsibility as human beings to develop the world under God (see Genesis 1:28). We are to be part of God's creative and redemptive work. We are called to be part of bringing the kingdom of God into every area of life.

---

3. Ibid., 35–42.
4. Ibid., 50.

Questions to reflect on might be:
- What significance does being part of God's creative order have on the decisions you make?
- What do the creative qualities of rational, righteous, responsible, restful, and relational mean for you?
- In what ways might your work be part of God's creative and redemptive work?

JESUS AS LEADER

Looking at the life and approach of Jesus gives a touchstone about how we might best approach our leadership role. Using a perspective on Jesus directly rather than using an articulation of Christian values as a starting point gives a human face to our role as leaders.

Some would say that Jesus is not a relevant role model in terms of the challenges we face as leaders, since he was pointing the way to the kingdom of God and identifying that he was the Son of God. He came to bring hope and, through his death, salvation—and therefore in the minds of some he was not sent to the world in order to be a great leader. Yet even if Jesus did not set out to be a major leader, the way he lived his life is highly relevant for leaders today in many spheres of life.

Some would say the fact that the cross was at the center of Jesus' purpose means that his life was far too tragic a role model for today's leaders. But many leaders go through their own "crucifixion" and "resurrection." Leaders can be created anew, strengthened, and enriched after being nailed in pain. Jesus pioneered a way through death to life that can be relevant to us too.

In my book *Mirroring Jesus as Leader*, I highlighted six aspects of Jesus' contribution as a leader: visionary, servant-leader, teacher, coach, radical, and healer. These themes are summarized below.

Jesus as Visionary

Although Jesus was an itinerant preacher, he could never be accused of aimless meandering. He had a strong sense of destiny. On one occasion when he was only twelve years old, he stayed behind in Jerusalem while his parents headed for home. Found talking with the scribes in the temple, Jesus was clear that he was going about his Father's business (see Luke 2:49). When he began his ministry, there was a purposefulness about his choice of disciples, his teaching, and the people with whom he interacted.

Jesus was clear sighted. His vision for the future kingdom of God intrigued, and to some extent inspired, his hearers. That vision certainly inspired the apostles and the early church. Jesus' personal vision involved the clarity of his purpose and the necessity of his death. He also had a vision in regard to his followers: he explicitly sent them into the world to preach the gospel.

Jesus was a visionary for his followers because he looked at the world and the way people live in a very different way. Achievements were based not on keeping the law but on demonstrating love.

Jesus as Servant-Leader

Jesus gave himself no special privileges. On the contrary, he even washed his disciples' feet. Servanthood was central to Jesus' ministry. He declared that "the Son of Man did not come to be served, but to serve" (Matthew 20:28). He emphasized that "whoever wants to become great among you must be your servant" (Matthew 20:26).

This servanthood was not a weak demonstration of a lack of will. Jesus' servanthood meant availability to those around him but not servitude to their whims. His servanthood was about generosity of spirit, not about blind obedience to the authorities.

The theme of servanthood occurs again and again in the Gospels. "Those who exalt themselves will be humbled" (Matthew 23:12).

"Whoever is least among you all is the greatest" (Luke 9:48). "Anyone who wants to be first must be the very last, and the servant of all" (Mark 9:35).

Jesus as Teacher

Great leaders, almost without exception, have written autobiographies or documents setting out their perspective. Jesus wrote no treatises or key documents. His impact was through his actions and his words. His teaching was primarily through stories, parables, and pictures. Sometimes his teaching was direct—for example, "Follow me"—but other times he stretched the thinking of his followers through his sayings and through his parables. The Sermon on the Mount is a classic demonstration of Jesus as teacher. For example, the Beatitudes were not precise instructions; they were statements that stretched the understanding of his hearers.

Jesus' aim was to enable his hearers to grow in their understanding and wisdom. He often did not give them precise answers because he respected their ability to think through what his words and parables meant in the practical living of their lives. As a teacher, Jesus could cope readily with one-to-one meetings, small groups, formal settings such as in a synagogue, and crowds in the open air. He was adaptable to the context of his audience. There were both frankness and generosity in his teaching. He focused on encouragement with some groups and on challenge with others. He accepted that his hearers would not understand his words the first time, so there was consistency in his message and the repetition of his themes in different stories and actions.

At the heart of Jesus' teaching was simplicity set against a background of many-faceted human interactions. The complexity of the Jewish law was encapsulated in the two commandments; he gave a wonderfully clear statement that held together loving God and loving your neighbor as yourself (Mark 12:30–31). This combined the teacher's gifts of clarity of vision and simplicity of message.

A number of Jesus' best-known phrases bring together vision, servanthood, and clarity as teacher. His injunction to "love your enemies, do good to those who hate you" (Luke 6:27) was simple in its vision, based on the servanthood of love and full of challenging simplicity.

Jesus as Coach

Jesus worked closely with a small group of disciples, identifying and developing their individual talents. He built his own team, but they were not people in his own mold. He constructed a team from different backgrounds. Fishermen and tax collectors would not be natural colleagues.

Jesus put his team in challenging leadership situations. He sent them out two by two; he threw them in the deep end. Jesus took a big risk considering how imperfectly the disciples had understood his message. But the disciples returned excited and surprised by what they had been able to do.

Jesus expected his disciples to develop their own articulation of the vision. When they did not understand, or could not keep awake, he was patient with them most of the time. He had to cope with one member of his team who became disaffected and poisonous. Jesus recognized the reality that teams often do not gel completely. He recognized that there would be dissent. He worked with James and John to stretch their understanding when they wanted to be first among the disciples. He did not chastise them—he challenged them (Mark 10:38).

The full benefit of the coaching Jesus gave his disciples became clear only after his ascension. He had worked with them for three years. Their progress was often three steps forward and two steps backward, but the groundwork had been laid. Once the disciples adjusted to Jesus' departure, the coaching that Jesus had given them was seen to be embedded in the strength of leadership of Peter, James, John, and the others.

Jesus as Radical

Jesus was unorthodox right from the start. Marked by his unorthodox parentage, being born in a stable, and having to flee to Egypt as a tiny baby, he was always likely to be a bit different. We do not know what sort of carpenter he was, but we do know that at a certain point in his life he made a major life change. He built an unorthodox team. He had a hugely varied network of friends and acquaintances and did not stick within one social setting. Jesus had an itinerant approach. He worked with people in different locations from different social backgrounds and with different perspectives. He was difficult to predict. He was constantly taking people by surprise.

Jesus was not radical for the sake of being radical. But he was not ashamed to be radical and stand up for what he believed. He took on the religious orthodox in debate. He changed the rules about the Sabbath. Jesus was radical in his approach, but he preserved the best of the traditions he inherited and could be gentle and kind in his manner. He could also be very direct in his words and in his actions; overturning the tables in the temple was the dramatic act of someone determined to make a difference. He was decisive and took bold actions. He was willing to break the mold both in the way he lived and in the way he died. Jesus' most dramatic actions followed periods of reflection.

Jesus as Healer

Jesus brought physical, emotional, and spiritual healing. He sought out the sick and the lame. He brought healing and new life. Sometimes his healing work was dramatic, for example, when he raised Jairus's daughter from the dead. At other times the healing was done quietly, as when the woman who just touched the hem of his garment felt his healing power flow into her.

Jesus brought emotional healing too. He helped sisters Mary and Martha understand their different perspectives and approaches. He brought healing and reassurance to the Samaritan woman at the well who felt like an outcast and had suffered from a series of broken relationships. Jesus' healing restored people to their communities; the healed leper was no longer an outcast. Jesus brought spiritual healing by renewing people's minds where hopelessness was replaced with a hope for the future. For Nicodemus and others, Jesus offered the newness of being born again into a new life.

I have often used the approach of inviting individuals to score themselves from 1 (not at all developed) to 5 (a major strength, lived out in reality) in respect to applying these aspects of Jesus' leadership. The figure below provides a possible self-assessment form.

Figure 1

	Your self-assessment	How others see you	Where you would like to be in one year	Your top two priority areas for development
Visionary				
Servant-Leader				
Teacher				
Coach				
Radical				
Healer				

As we have identified some areas for development, the following sets out, under each theme, an illustration from the life of Jesus and then some practical questions.

Jesus as Visionary

Jesus set out a vision of a world in which blessed or happy are the poor in spirit, those who mourn, the meek, those who hunger and thirst for righteousness, the merciful, the pure in heart, the peacemakers, and those who are persecuted because of righteousness (Matthew 5:3–12). His vision was not about precise productivity outputs but about the nature of relationship and the respect in which people are held.

- Do you have a picture of the type of community you are trying to build? What is the place in that community for people, for the poor in spirit?
- Can you separate your short-term priorities from your long-term vision? Do you always leave enough space to take those actions that will help deliver the vision in the longer term?

Jesus as Servant-Leader

Jesus took his disciples by surprise when he poured water into a basin and began to wash their feet. Peter said, "No, you shall never wash my feet." Jesus answered, "Unless I wash you, you have no part with me" (John 13:8). Peter's response then was to ask that not only his feet but also his hands and head be washed. Jesus' exhortation to the disciples was, "Now that I, your Lord and Teacher, have washed your feet, you also should wash one another's feet" (John 13:14). This was a very visual and practical demonstration of the leader as servant caring for others. Jesus was authentic because he led by example. This helped Peter come to a new insight about the nature of leadership.

- What does being a servant-leader mean for you?
- How can you best serve the people who work for you?

Jesus as Teacher

Jesus was questioned by a rich young man who said, "Teacher, what good thing must I do to get eternal life?" (Matthew 19:16). Jesus expressed warmth to the young man but still challenged him at the deepest level. As teacher, Jesus was available to the rich young man; he listened to him carefully and discussed his situation. Jesus recognized that the young man had lived the Ten Commandments. He challenged him. He drew lessons through visual pictures, and he concluded with some memorable phrases that stuck in the minds of his hearers.

- Are you willing to listen to understand fully where people are coming from and let that shape how you encourage them to view the future?
- As a teacher, how can you best help focus individuals on values and behaviors that are the most important in terms of respecting individual dignity and difference?

Jesus as Coach

In the final chapter of his Gospel, John relayed the story of Jesus challenging Peter with a series of personal questions. Jesus asked Peter if he loved him more than the others around him. After asking Peter the question a second time, Jesus said, "Take care of my sheep" (John 21:16). The picture of the relationship between Jesus and Peter is one of openness, trust, and challenge. Jesus forgave Peter and reinstated him, but he did check out what he had learned.

- Do you get close enough to the people you lead? Do you set aside time to have one-to-one discussions?
- Do you think enough about how the people you are working with can best grow in wisdom? How can you, as a leader, best coach those individuals?

Jesus as Radical

When Jesus entered the temple and found people "buying and selling," he became indignant and began driving them out (Mark 11:15). Jesus was continually challenging the authorities. As we have seen, he reframed the commandments into the two overarching commandments about loving God and loving your neighbor (Mark 12:30–31).

- Are you willing to be frank about unfairness and ill treatment and intervene when immoral or unlawful actions are taking place?

- Are you robust in identifying the need for change to improve the community within an organization and willing to come up with positive proposals to effect that change?

Jesus as Healer

Jesus healed physically, emotionally, and spiritually. He enabled people to return to their communities. Sometimes the healing was in public, sometimes in private. He spoke to the whole person, not just to physical needs.

- How can you best bring healing to individuals for whom you have a responsibility?
- How can you best bring healing within an organization, irrespective of who might have caused the pain?

Taking account of the cultural context is important. Francis Chung, who is based in Vancouver and works in a global commercial business, suggests that in the Eastern context Jesus as a visionary resonates well, but Jesus as a servant and coach might resonate less well. In the Eastern world there is more formality, and the boss is expected to behave as the boss. Hence the leader as parent rather than peer can resonate more effectively in the East.

In his recent book, *The Fourfold Leadership of Jesus*, Andrew Watson, the bishop of Aston, expresses his wariness about the attempt to "baptize" secular management theories and to see Jesus as the ultimate CEO. He points to a debate that can polarize Christians between those who are "doing" and those in favor of simply "being." Imitating Christ cannot dispense with the need for spiritual discipline (being with Jesus), but neither can it ignore the challenge of the practical living out of the Christian gospel.[5]

---

5.   Andrew Watson, *The Fourfold Leadership of Jesus* (Abingdon, UK: Barnabas, 2008), 12ff.

Watson says that Jesus virtually never talked about leadership. The language in the New Testament is of *disciples* (literally, "learners") or *apostles* ("those who are sent"). He says that Jesus never gave his followers any description that smacked of leadership in its normal sense or took them aside specifically for leadership training. He never passed on to them explicit insights regarding vision seeking, team building, or time management. From Jesus the disciples learned about the kingdom of God, about humility and prayer, money and generosity, love and purity. From him they learned about forgiveness and grace, healing and proclamation, heaven and hell.[6]

Watson summarizes the fourfold leadership of Jesus—*come, follow, wait,* and *go*—in the following way:

Come to me suggests a leader who is facing his or her people, arms perhaps outstretched in a gesture of friendliness and warmth. Acceptance and accessibility are the key themes of such an approach, as leaders consciously seek to reduce the distance between themselves and those they lead. *Come to me,* therefore, is strongly relational.

The call *Follow me,* by contrast, implies leaders who are walking ahead of their people, with only their backs (not their faces) in view to those responding to the challenge. The ability to inspire is foundational to the *Follow me* leader, but it is inspiration based on actions, not just words.

Disciples are called to *Wait for me* and be held in that place by a sense of expectation, trust, or simple need. *Wait for me* leadership, at its best, is faithful, prayerful, and patient, and it encourages the same qualities in others.

Go for me presents the image of a disciple looking out toward the horizon and the leader standing beside the disciple with one hand on his or her shoulder and the other hand pointing out the direction in which the disciple needs to go. It forms the substance of missionary calling,

---

6.   Ibid., 12.

inviting people to step away from their home-based comforts and securities and set out on a journey that is, by its nature, both exciting and scarily unpredictable.[7]

When I have discussed with various people the six themes in my book *Mirroring Jesus as Leader* and the perspective from Andrew Watson, two additional characteristics have frequently been referred to: *availability* and *patience*. Jesus made himself available to a wide range of different people. He stopped to talk to the woman who touched the hem of his garment. He went to tea with Zacchaeus. When the crowds followed Jesus, he spent time with them. Jesus made sure he had periods when he was alone or just with his disciples, but he was regularly available to a wider group to listen, to talk, and to bring healing.

For Andrew Watson, a sense of waiting is not like the inactivity of the two tramps in *Waiting for Godot* who fill their days with increasingly meaningless chatter as they wait for someone who might save them and fulfill their lives. He comments, "Nothing could be further removed from the biblical call to 'wait for the Lord' or from the faith-filled expectancy that lies at its heart. Waiting in this sense is both an expression of our dependence on God and the recognition that his timing is not always our timing. If we are to live (and lead) properly, we must do so for the longer term rather than seeking first a quick win and a popularity that will evaporate as quickly as it has materialised."[8]

Figure 2 sets out some very telling responses I received when I asked a range of leaders in different sectors and countries about the insights from Jesus that are most relevant for them as a leader. The life of Christ is inspirational for all these individuals. They see Jesus' actions as providing key touchstones for the way they live out their leadership roles.

---

7.   Ibid., 19.
8.   Ibid., 99.

Figure 2

INSIGHTS FROM JESUS FOR LEADERS

"Christ is a great role model. He had hope in people who seemed dead. You should not get tired of people, as Jesus did not get tired of people. Jesus spent most of his time with the poor and the homeless and not that much time with thinkers."—*business consultant*

"I have always found Jesus to be inspirational. He did not need to negotiate. He created new belief alongside reasons for belief." —*senior executive*

"Jesus brings a clear understanding of what whole life is like. There is the importance of the forty days in the wilderness. He is engaging with friendly forces and then he gets to critical moments. He goes to the enemy camp. He understands his mission. He fights his campaigns. He does not let himself be thrown off course." —*senior military leader*

"Jesus had a great ability to detach himself, to retreat to the mountains. There was, for Jesus, time to refresh. He found time to be on his own. We do not always recognize how radical he was. He was innovative in his time. He was open to the disciples; reconciliation was important to him. We often think that success is based on others' failures. Success is about building other people up too. There is a judgment theme and an accountability theme. He was bold and tough about priorities, but there was compassion too." —*national politician*

"The availability theme is so important. God is personal and incarnate and talks to human beings. Jesus could make people feel they were the only person who mattered. There was a strong sense of love and personal connection. He was associated with people and listened to people. His influence did not fit into anyone's presumption of who he should be." —*HR director*

"Jesus brought a single-minded approach to mission. He knew he was going to the cross. Satan tried to take him off track, which would have been bypassing the cross. In the wilderness there was a single-minded focus on mission and reliance on the Father. He was courageous in the relationship with the Pharisees. He faced them down on a regular basis. He never backed down once." —*military leader*

"There was a quiet firmness. Jesus had firm, clear views with simple, clear messages. He didn't put things across in a threatening way." —*finance director*

"Jesus was available to his disciples. They could discuss things with him. He allowed dialogue and had patience with them. He withdrew and let people come and talk with him. He communicated in different ways with different people. He understood the doubts that Thomas had and went straight to meet his needs. He had an awareness of Peter's character. He saw the potential in people. In sending out the disciples there was practical instruction. There was always complete practicality about what he did." —*private sector leader*

The perspectives of individuals vary as they identify with those aspects of Jesus as leader that resonate most with them in their situation. It isn't surprising that military leaders refer to Jesus having a single-minded focus and not allowing himself to be thrown off course, or that a politician refers to the balance between being bold and tough together with the need for compassion, or that a human resources director and a private sector leader refer to human connection with people and the ability to see their potential.

Identifying with the aspects of Jesus' leadership that resonate most with you is a powerful way of embedding the approach of Jesus in the way you live. There is, however, an important test of objectivity. We must avoid creating God in our own image and defining Jesus by our own preferences. Keeping a clear focus on who Jesus was and what he did may well mean challenging rather than endorsing our preferred approach.

Some questions to reflect on might be:

- What aspects of Jesus as leader resonate most with you?
- What aspects of what you observe about the leadership of Jesus do you want to embrace more?
- As a result, what are some practical next steps you could take over the next few weeks?
- What does living in obedience to God over the next phase of your life mean for you?

LIVING THE CHRISTIAN THEMES

I invited perspectives from a number of different groups of people about what they think are the great Christian themes that are relevant in the work context. Frequently mentioned themes included service, stewardship, humility, sound judgment, dependability, forgiveness, compassion, generosity, enabling others, self-sacrifice, excellence, boldness, kindness, encouragement, approachability, and respecting diversity.

Jesus saw the intrinsic worth in all people and accepted individuals as they were. God sees everyone as intrinsically valuable. Hence all these themes start with viewing people in a positive light as creatures of God. Christians are encouraged to be transformed by the renewing of their minds, thus the encouragement to take forward these Christians themes in the work context. Perspectives from Christian leaders in the global workplace on each of these themes include:

Service

"Bring thanks and gratefulness as an opportunity for service. Be grateful for what you have got; do not be angry about what you have not got."—*business consultant*

Stewardship

"Stewardship is a crucial part of my faith, and it is also highly relevant to my work responsibilities. I want to leave the organization in better shape than I found it. Stewardship means always taking the longer view."—*chief executive*

Humility

"I never say I'm doing a great job."—*chief executive*

"Being humble is important. I work hard not to have an ego and not to have myself at the center of what I do. Putting up with others' bad behavior is a challenge, as most people are driven by their own personal ego, but being able to stand back and try to reflect on the humility of Jesus is important."—*private sector leader*

"Knowing that you do not have all the answers, as well as always being willing to listen thoughtfully to others, is important."—*finance director*

"Humility is crucial. Sometimes it is saying, 'I do not know the answers.' Sometimes it is saying, 'I've got it wrong.'"—*national politician*

Sound Judgment

"Sound judgment flows from recognizing that you have a choice."—*HR director*

"Sound judgment is linked to integrity. It means making decisions responsibly and then being willing to admit you have gotten it wrong sometimes. It is being willing to listen and reevaluate in the light of further research."—*military leader*

Dependability

"The ability to be relied upon is central to building a firm reputation. When you say you are going to do something, credibility then depends on ensuring you do it."—*national politician*

"Dependability is recognizing that you have been put there for a reason and then serving the people well."—*HR director*

Forgiveness

"Forgiveness is central to moving on. It is quite hard sometimes. It is particularly hard when you feel you have been let down."—*chief executive*

"Jesus' forgiveness was crucial. You are not to be like the world. Being different and forgiving is not being a doormat. I met an IRA [separatist Irish Republican Army] guy recently, and listening to his story was important. Understanding the life journeys of other people is always important."—*military leader*

"Giving people the opportunity to fail is important. It is giving people the opportunity for a second chance that is a distinguishing feature of a leader."—*national politician*

"People sometimes see my role in HR as a soft option. Some approach me with extreme anger. You have to calm them down. I am neither hurt nor damaged by them. I forgive them and turn the other cheek. Christian values are part of my DNA. There is a key theme of moral integrity. If you are morally bankrupt, there is no integrity; hence the importance of forgiveness."—*HR director*

"Because of the speed with which we need to make decisions, there will be mistakes. The theme of the need to move faster is being pressed upon us, but that needs to be linked with being forgiving when there are mistakes."—*finance director*

"I always try to forgive. You do not hold a grudge, but you do sometimes have to dismiss people. You are caring for the whole of the organization."—*chief executive*

Compassion

"There needs to be an underlying compassion for the customers you are dealing with. Bringing an ethos of basic decency for prisoners is strong. It is important to have a very strong sense of treating people with proper decency."—*finance director in a government organization*

"Compassion has led me to work on professional standards and complaints about the police. There is a line beyond which you cannot help people—for example, when they are being dishonest—but sometimes there is a feeling of 'There but for the grace of God, go I.' Compassion is about enabling people to have a second chance, except when there is dishonesty, malice, or deceit."—*senior police leader*

"Compassion is about not always being hard nosed, but sometimes you have to be bold where the compassionate thing is to sack someone. Compassion is relevant in not countenancing unjustified action. It doesn't mean being soft. There is a boldness about compassion."—*finance specialist*

"Compassion should not be confused with bad business judgment."—*senior international banker*

Generosity

"Generosity is about working effectively through others. Sometimes there is a tendency to work around the theme of 'I told you so.' The best thing is to bite your tongue. Generosity can also be about not taking the credit when other people need a boost of recognition."—*finance director*

"Generosity must be about individual judgment about what is right, having taken into account all the views of the different stakeholders."—*chief executive*

Enabling Others

"My job is making others feel great. I need to draw out and develop talent through bringing an enabler role."—*national politician*

"I am called to make the most of human potential. The human condition has been lifted through the incarnation. It is my job to bring a strong sense of human value to enable individuals to make the most of their potential."—*HR director*

"It is not Christian to be tied to self. Our priority is enabling achievement by others as well."—*private sector leader*

Self-sacrifice

"I spend a lot of time dealing with corporate responsibility. We are heavily involved in working with local communities. We are going to an African country for a week as a management team. We are heavily involved in environmental stewardship. Self-sacrifice is about leading by example. When we build lavatories in Africa, we may be sleeping in mud huts. It is really important for me to do this and to be seen doing this."—*private sector leader*

Excellence

"The Christian should aspire to excellence. The Christian should watch any abrogation of leadership. In the Book of Zechariah success was measured in different ways. Gideon had to leave many of his army behind, but he was still successful. Success is not about building the right army, as some would view it."—*military leader*

Boldness

"There is a need to be bold and take risks sometimes. You need the confidence, if an action does not work, to restrain from blaming others or yourself too much. You need the confidence that the people will then still treat you fairly, even when boldness doesn't work."—*finance director*

"Boldness is not about doing things just for the sake of doing them."—*senior international banker*

"Boldness is about treating everyone equally. It is recognizing the difficulties when you have to arbitrate, but ensuring fair resolutions."—*private sector leader*

Kindness

"Kindness is one of the most underrated qualities in the Western world. A moment of kindness can make such a difference. It is linked to courtesy. Most of us remember a note from an individual. Kindness might be writing a personal note every day to someone who has done a good job."—*national politician*

Encouragement

"Encouragement is about listening to the positive perspective of others and not allowing yourself to be disheartened. The overall theme is grace. God is with us. Grace brings the richness of God into human life."—*HR director*

"Having a sense of communion and celebration with others leads to encouragement."—*private sector executive*

Approachability

"What differentiates leaders is the heart and passion. The effective leader has to have the passion to seek a way forward and the passion to succeed. What differentiates leaders is the type of passion, purpose, and motivation that leads to being available for other people."—*private sector leader*

"As a senior police officer I am in a powerful position. I make real efforts to balance out power relations, but the power issue never goes away. My operating style is that I do not need to apply that power directly all that often. While recognizing the hierarchy in relationships, it is important that I aim to be approachable."—*senior police leader*

Respecting Diversity

"Respecting diversity is so important. When Jesus was at the well he treated the Samaritan woman with great respect. He mixed with publicans and sinners. He lived a life of diversity."—*senior international banker*

The perspectives above came from individuals wrestling honestly with applying the great Christian themes to the context of their workplace. Their frankness and honesty are of particular encouragement to me.

These comments represent the tip of the iceberg. The Christian themes infuse the whole being of the thoughtful Christian—not just those aspects visible to others. All the themes above are likely to be evident in some way in all Christian leaders. There will always be a strong sense of service, whether spoken or unspoken. Humility and sound judgment will always need to sit alongside each other. Dependability will be a hallmark of a Christian leader.

Many of these themes will characterize good leaders whether or not they possess a faith perspective. But a central place for forgiveness and compassion may well begin to identify the Christian leader as bringing a distinctive approach, especially when linked to generosity and self-sacrifice. Boldness can sometimes be lacking, just as humility and self-sacrifice—taken to extremes—can limit the effectiveness of the Christian leader. Central to any Christian leader is approachability and respect for diversity.

Let me encourage you to reflect on the following:

- Which of the Christian themes above resonate the most with you?
- Which two do you think you do well and represent your strengths?
- Which two would you like to develop further?
- What might be your next steps in taking forward these two themes?

In an interview with John Mao, a lawyer from Vancouver, he commented that we have to realize that the ultimate goal for many is money. "We have to recognize that we live in a commercial world in terms of where other people are coming from. It does mean you have to give a bit sometimes. Humility is important. Arrogant approaches get in the way and can be a hindrance. But a bottom line should be a bottom line.

When you make a compromise, you give up on things rather than giving up on principles."

Sometimes different themes seem in apparent contradiction to one another. On some occasions we have a strong sense of the importance of being bold and clear, and at other times forgiveness seems to be the right next step. The next section looks at the interplay between toughness and forgiveness.

WHEN IS TOUGHNESS OR FORGIVENESS THE RIGHT CHRISTIAN RESPONSE?

Is describing somebody as tough a compliment or a criticism? The word *tough* has in it the hint of being a bit on the negative side. Major Bagstock, in Charles Dickens's *Dombey and Son*, comments, "He's tough, Ma'am, tough, is J. B. Tough and devilish sly!"

When we hear somebody say that George is tough on his wife, that sounds like a bad sort of toughness. If we hear that George is tough on his children, that may be good or it may be bad. If we hear that George is tough in his training schedule in preparation for running the marathon, that sounds like a good sort of toughness.

There is no reference to *tough* or *toughness* in this context in a Bible concordance. But the words are in common usage today in instances where toughness has a good side to it. In the 1990s the UK Labour Party built a lot of credit by using the phrase "tough on crime and tough on the causes of crime." "Tough love" is advocated as a quality for which both managers and parents should aspire. To be "tough but tender" is regarded as a positive attribute.

The word *toughness* may have too much of a macho ring to it to be immediately attractive to Christians. The Christian leader needs to be tough but also needs to know the boundaries of that toughness. If you have somebody working for you who is letting his or her colleagues and staff down, the first reaction is to support and help this individual and to nurture him or her back into effectiveness. But what about the risk that this person could be doing damage to other people during the intervening period? To be fair to one person and give him or her the opportunity to improve might be grossly unfair to others who are suffering because of this individual's inadequate leadership. This illustration is at the heart of the dilemma as to how tough the Christian leader should be.

We are enjoined to love our neighbors as ourselves (Matthew 19:19). But in loving one neighbor we could appear to another neighbor to be completely failing in living out this principle.

What lessons can we draw from the life of Jesus about how tough the Christian leader should be?

- **Jesus was tough on himself.** He had a rigorous traveling schedule, he withdrew to the desert, he fasted, and he was willing to sacrifice his life on the cross. But while being tough on himself, he also allowed a woman to pour expensive perfume on his feet, he enjoyed the hospitality of many different people, and he ensured that there was plenty of wine to drink at a wedding feast.
- **Jesus was tough on his disciples.** He expected them to leave their homes and follow him. They put up with an itinerant lifestyle. He sent them out two by two on training exercises. He trained them hard. He sometimes let them know when they had not lived up to his expectations.
- **Jesus often appeared tough on his family.** He was not at home much when he went journeying with his disciples. He put his family into a wider context of God's love for everyone. But at critical moments he was there for his mother, asking his disciple John to look after her when he was on the cross (John 19:25–27).
- **Jesus was tough with the individuals with whom he debated faith and life.** He expected individual leaders who came to him, such as Nicodemus, to be willing to change their approach. He listened to the scribes and Pharisees; he debated with them and spoke up when he disagreed.
- **Jesus was tough in his use of time.** Reading the Gospels,

you sense there was something deliberate in the way Jesus used his time. He gave a lot of time to his disciples and allowed time for the crowds, but he also set aside time to be alone and to be with the small group of Peter, James, and John. Jesus would deliberately move away from people who needed his healing and wanted to hear his words in order to be alone or with a small group of disciples. He was making tough decisions on how he used his time and prioritizing in a clear way, even though it meant disappointing some individuals.

What are the parallels from the life of Jesus for us as leaders? His was not a 9-to-5 vocation. He was highly focused on his Father's business. He put demanding expectations upon himself. He had a rigorous traveling schedule, lived with demanding expectations, and ensured there were moments when he withdrew to the desert. It is sometimes too easy as Christians just to assume that if we pray, everything will be all right. Christian leaders are likely to be tough on themselves, but that needs to be kept within the context that work is only one part of life—not the be-all and end-all—as they live out God's calling in different aspects of their lives.

It may seem simplistic to draw a comparison between Jesus and his disciples and us and our staff. But there are relevant principles. It is perfectly consistent with a picture of Jesus as manager to expect staff members to work hard, to encourage them to grow and develop, and to expect them to take on new experiences. The balance of challenge and encouragement is important for the Christian leader, as is that sense of forgiveness if our staff members don't get it right the first time.

In regard to our families, perhaps we can take comfort from the fact that Jesus was pretty tough on his family members in terms of the amount of time he spent with them. But there was quality time at key moments. It is all too obvious to see the ill effects when a Christian leader who is also a church leader leaves too little time for family: therein lies the roots of teenage rebellion.

The Christian can easily be viewed as a soft touch when it comes to negotiating or building partnerships. Toughness in negotiation may be no less important for the Christian leader than for other leaders. Effective negotiation that is based on clarity and trust can be done just as well by a Christian as anyone else. On some occasions it can be easier because of the importance the Christian attaches to building a strong basis for trust. One of the toughest things for leaders to do is to admit when they are wrong and change their minds. The apostle Paul is a perfect example of someone who was willing to listen and then change direction (Acts 16:6–10).

Maybe the toughest thing for managers is how they use their time. Reflecting Jesus' priorities puts an emphasis on time for your direct reports, time for wider visibility and communication, and also time to be alone. The impression is of Jesus using his time well—a robust challenge to us to use our time in a tough and effective way.

So what is the relevance of all of this to life as a Christian leader in a busy world, be it in a hospital, a school, or an office? Toughness is not macho, but it is disciplined, purposeful, and based on listening and clear thinking. John was a Christian in a senior position in a security firm. As demands for the firm's work went up or down, he was expected to recruit or dismiss workers. He accepted this as an inevitable part of the job. When an individual's contract needed to come to an end, John always made time to talk one to one in a private space. He never dismissed people through a text message but instead engaged them in a constructive discussion about what might be their best next steps.

As a naval officer, James knew he had to have different relationships with people at different points of time. When he was on the bridge at four o'clock in the morning, there could be philosophical conversations when he would talk about what mattered to him in his life, including his faith. At other moments it would be more command and control. Both aspects of the relationship were important to him. The fact that there were occasions when it was right to talk about his faith did not dilute the importance of toughness when that was necessary to do the job effectively.

For Sophie, an HR manager, her toughness came from believing strongly in the message from the parable of the talents. The employees who just wanted to hide their talents away were not going to be employee of the month. The thrust for her, as a Christian HR manager, was to expect each individual to be developing his or her talents well.

Christian leaders are tough and fair in the leadership of their staff, and it is clear where the boundaries are. Every staff member has a life beyond the workplace. The Christian manager wants to ensure that the employee's energy is not so sapped that they cannot enjoy life outside the workplace. Putting so much pressure on people that their energy is sucked dry is not acceptable in the long term, and even in the short term is only tolerable in exceptional circumstances, if at all.

Sometimes Christian leaders will need to communicate to HR or their senior managers that certain practices need to be altered because of unfairness. Tough feedback is a reasonable expectation. Feedback, done well, can be a most precious gift. The Christian leader should not be afraid of tough feedback that is thoughtful, measured, and purposeful.

Where Does Forgiveness Fit In?

Jesus said to his disciples that they should forgive not seven times, but seventy times seven times (Matthew 18:22). What is the relevance of this to a manager with a clear requirement to deliver outcomes in which all the team members need to make a full contribution and there is no room for people to make mistakes? Do you "forgive" the police sergeant who is not doing his job effectively and is not getting a grip on local crime? Forgiving the police sergeant may mean an elderly woman in his beat gets mugged, whereas if he had done his job properly, then she might not have gotten mugged.

To a manager, forgiveness is important. Individuals need the opportunity to test out different approaches. They must be allowed to fail in order to succeed later. But to a leader, forgiveness does depend on a willingness to improve performance. I would not be "loving my neighbor" if I kept forgiving the police sergeant who showed no will to improve his performance. For a leader, forgiveness is vital, but it needs to be matched by a willingness to improve performance. Balancing "forgiveness" and "loving my neighbor" is one of the challenges Jesus gave his followers.

Where Does Fairness Fit In?

Sometimes we can be so preoccupied with one individual that we fail to see the consequential effects on others. Decisions are not always straightforward.

- Is it fair to promote a loyal employee when going to the open market may produce someone who will do a better job?
- Is it fair to invest in a new recruit with a long career ahead of him or her over someone not far from retirement who needs to be encouraged?
- Do you sense that sometimes you are tougher on some people than others because you are influenced by how much you like or dislike them?

For a leader, effective toughness involves clarity and compassion: clarity in regard to the utter objectivity in the way we view people and situations, and compassion in regard to being able to walk in someone else's shoes and see issues from his or her perspective.

Managing Necessary Staff Reductions

How would you face a situation where you are asked to reduce the number of your staff by 20 percent? (Running away is not an acceptable answer!) A good approach to your management responsibilities in this situation might be

- to understand the reasons for the decision;
- to know what help will be available to those who are let go;
- to be clear about the next steps and to communicate those steps in an open, honest, and fair way;
- to provide time for conversations with the affected people and then to listen to them empathetically—without being unduly swayed by special pleading, as that would be unfair to other people;
- to maintain strict objectivity in taking the decision forward while being compassionate and caring for those directly affected, as shown in the time and support you provide for them; and
- to balance effectively your responsibilities to both the people who are staying and those who are going.

Being part of an organization and having an important influence within it demand toughness of mind and action. We cannot avoid tough decisions. What is crucial is how we make them and whether we are able to do so in a way that is consistent with our faith and perspective. Loving our neighbor as ourselves demands a personal toughness in relation to ourselves before we can legitimately be tough in relation to others. But we should not shy away from being tough. We are called not to court popularity but to bring the love and values of Jesus into all our dealings as a manager.

There is a marked difference in the approach needed to work well with volunteers compared with employees. The volunteer can just walk away. With the employee there is more of a mutual obligation and a financial accountability. But the principles about the need for clarity and compassion still apply. Much depends on the nature of the contract, or understanding, between the manager and the volunteer. But for volunteers to be most effective, clarity of role and acceptance that tough decisions may be needed are important elements of success.

Drawing on My Personal Experience

I would like to draw on two strands of my own personal experience, first from my work as a director general within government and second as an executive coach. In a succession of different jobs within government, I would say that I was tough on myself, pretty tough in relation to the people with whom I dealt, and variable in terms of toughness in my use of time. But I was not always as tough as I should have been in relation to some of the people who worked for me. I deliberately gave people the benefit of the doubt most of the time. In retrospect, however, that was not always in their best interest or in mine. Sometimes I should have been tougher, for people's own good.

In Micah 6:8, the prophet is clear about what the Lord requires of his people: "To act justly and to love mercy and to walk humbly with your God." Acting justly (i.e., being tough) sits alongside loving mercy (i.e., forgiveness). But it also sits alongside walking humbly with your God (i.e., humility).

As Christians, we are under God's authority. God is tough on us, his children. He purifies us with fire (1 Peter 1:7), but he will not test us beyond what we are able to bear (1 Corinthians 10:13). God gives us hope where there is darkness. There are parallels here: as a Christian leader we may sometimes need to "purify with fire," but never to the point where those we lead are tested beyond what they are able to bear. We can do this in an understanding and compassionate way only if we know well our people's skills, abilities, and emotional makeup.

Toughness is not of itself a good or an evil. The issue is how it is used and the context in which it is applied. Toughness is normally going to be a virtue and only occasionally a vice. But if toughness borders on foolhardiness, it may be time to think again.

Some practical questions to reflect on here:

- In what ways was Jesus a tough leader? How did he balance clarity and compassion?
- What two lessons do you draw from the experience of Jesus as a tough leader that are relevant to you?
- Where does forgiveness fit in? How often should you forgive people who are letting themselves and their colleagues down?
- How does fairness apply in the way you make tough decisions?
- Can you be tough and tender, clear and compassionate, at the same time?
- What is the relevance to you, in the workplace, of the requirement "to act justly and to love mercy and to walk humbly with your God"?

EMBEDDING THE FRUIT OF THE SPIRIT

Paul wrote to the Galatians that "it is for freedom that Christ has set us free" (Galatians 5:1). The Galatians were encouraged to serve one another humbly in love, in keeping the command "Love your neighbor as yourself" (Galatians 5:14). The fruit of the Spirit is described as "love, joy, peace, patience, kindness, goodness, faithfulness, gentleness and self-control" (Galatians 5:22–23). This is not a list of soft, cozy attributes. Living each of them requires persistence and energy, as well as acceptance that we will not always get it right.

Here are questions to reflect on in respect to each aspect of the fruit of the Spirit:

Love

- How much love are you prepared to show to an individual who is undermining you?
- When does tough love demand a clear and critical response?

- What should you do when any sense of love for particular individuals seems to be wearing thin?

Joy

- How deep is the level of joy within the teams for which you are responsible?
- Is joy something you can encourage and nurture more in others?
- How can you allow a sense of joy to be more obviously present in your own life?

Peace

- When do you feel the greatest sense of peace within yourself, and how can you nurture that?
- What is the next step in your faith journey that will enable you to be more at peace with yourself?
- How can you bring a greater sense of harmony to others?

Patience

- Are you self-aware enough to know when your patience is likely to be exhausted?
- In what areas do you want to increase your capacity to show patience?

Kindness

- Who has shown great kindness to you, and what has been the impact of that upon you?
- What acts of kindness are difficult for you to initiate?
- How can showing kindness become a joy rather than a trial?

Goodness

- What brings out the best of goodness in you?
- How can you ensure that goodness gets a prominent place in the way you think and act?

- How can you ensure that your goodness is not trite (and therefore meaningless)?

Faithfulness

- Who are the main encouragers to you in terms of faithfulness?
- What has faithfulness meant to you over the last year?
- What might be your next steps in growing in faithfulness?

Gentleness

- When are you most gentle?
- Who brings out gentleness in you, and how can you extend its effectiveness?
- How might you become more gentle and yet firm at the same time?

Self-Control

- What lessons can you draw from occasions when your self-control has not been what you wanted it to be?
- Do you sometimes judge yourself too harshly in regard to self-control?
- How can you best put in place frameworks that enable you to keep your level of self-control where you want it to be?

In all these areas there is a balance as we recognize our strengths and weaknesses—that is, believing that God's love upholds us while at the same time acknowledging our frailties. It is important that we don't beat ourselves up by being excessively self-critical as we evaluate ourselves according to the fruit of the Spirit. Even the greatest saints did not necessarily reach perfection. We are bound to live within our limitations.

Rather than beating ourselves up, we can celebrate that one aspect of the fruit of the Spirit is *joy*. Seeking joy in even the smallest things can provide us with a sense of encouragement. Henri Nouwen says this about joy:

Joy is what makes life worth living, but for many, joy seems hard to find. They complain that their lives are sorrowful and depressing. What then brings the joy we so much desire? Are some people just lucky, while others have run out of luck? Strange as it may sound, we can choose joy. Two people can be part of the same event, but one may choose to live it quite differently from the other. One may choose to trust that what happened, painful as it may be, holds a promise. The other may choose despair and be destroyed by it. What makes us human is precisely this freedom of choice.[9]

UNDERSTANDING HUMAN NATURE

Paul also exhorted the Galatians to keep in step with the Spirit and not to become conceited, provoking and envying each other (Galatians 5:25–26). The apostle referred to a range of behaviors flowing from our sinful nature, which can include sexual immorality, hatred, discord, jealousy, rage, selfish ambition, dissension, and envy (Galatians 5:19–21).

Understanding human nature is about understanding ourselves, our loved ones, and the people with whom we are working. Sometimes we have to be very clear about how we can best protect ourselves from our own frailties. Key questions might be:

- In what areas are you most at risk of not meeting the standards that are most important to you?
- How can you best ensure that you keep the right equilibrium so that the risks are kept to a minimum?
- Are you aware of the trigger points that let you know when you need to take corrective action?
- Who are your best sources of support and encouragement to ensure that you keep your cool and your calm?

---

9.   Henri Nouwen, *Bread for the Journey* (London: Darton, Longman and Todd, 1996), 38.

- What aspects of your practice of living faith best protect you from yourself when you are at risk of not living up to what you believe is appropriate behavior?

Bob knew that he was at risk in some circumstances of losing his cool and becoming angry. For a long while he had fought this sense of anger and had become very cross with himself when it had been displayed. He comforted himself by recalling that Jesus had shown anger in the temple—and for good reason! Bob used various techniques to try to control his anger. What seemed to work best was a combination of taking a deep breath while trying to take a step back, seeing the person he was angry with as a child of God, attempting to look beyond the immediate issue, and drinking a glass of water. When Bob was able to use a combination of techniques that held his anger in balance, he celebrated by smiling to himself.

A sense of confession was important for Sharon. At times she felt her envious nature was an influence for good since it drove her to make a positive difference. But envy crept up on her much more often than she wanted, whether it was about someone's car, house, or clothes. Articulating her own private words of confession was important to her, alongside doing it as part of corporate worship on a weekly basis. Understanding our own human nature is part of living our lives before God in an open, powerful, confessional, and joyful way.

Understanding human nature is also about understanding the nature of others. So often individuals and teams start off with good intentions, and then problems appear. The willingness to be collegial and mutually supportive can soon dissipate if ambition or personal priorities erode a shared sense of common endeavor.

Bringing a Christian presence is not standing idly by. On many occasions it will be about being supportive and "nipping problems in the bud." Sometimes it will mean firm action and facing up to issues so that individuals do not get away with behavior that is undermining others.

This can mean showing compassion through the use of firm language so that small problems do not gradually become major issues.

Margaret always wanted her own way. Judith, a colleague, not wanting to embarrass Margaret, was discreet enough to seek a private conversation. She was complimentary about many aspects of what Margaret was doing. Once Margaret was smiling, Judith gently drew her attention to the perception that many people had about Margaret always wanting her own way and the negative effect that had on others. Judith's message, given with gentleness and compassion, began to have an effect. It was an excellent example of combining firm action with words chosen in a thoughtful and sensitive way.

A Christian will always want to see the good in people, which thereby provides a sound basis for bringing encouragement and motivation. The danger is that the Christian may be oblivious of some deep-seated problems. I can remember working with two different individuals at different stages of my career who always expressed positive intent but never quite delivered. I believed they would make progress, but neither of them did so. In both cases it was not until quite late in the day that I recognized there was an alcohol dependency. Once I understood the situation, the pattern of behavior was clear. It may not have been possible to help either of them, but if I had recognized the symptoms earlier, it might have been feasible to have taken some action.

Fraud or financial misdemeanor can easily be slipped into, even if in modest ways. The Christian response might be a combination of

- rigorous accountability arrangements to limit the scope for misuse;
- clear action when there are signs of a problem; and
- decisiveness and understanding in ensuring that problems are not allowed to recur.

Understanding human nature is about bringing both compassion and objectivity. It is applying practical wisdom and not being taken in by manipulation, which can distort even the most balanced of people.

GROWING SELF-AWARENESS

Ensuring that you have a good level of self-awareness is accepting that you are God's unique creature. Self-awareness comes through our own experience, the feedback of others, and allowing Scripture and prayer to impact us.

Sometimes our values and backgrounds can be a source of distortion. Might there be something quite rigid about aspects of the Christian background from which we come or the cultural baggage that gets in the way? Our beliefs and emotions can produce a powerful cocktail that can send us off on a particular direction that we might regard as misdirected if we had reflected more and sought the counsel of others more.

Emotions such as disappointment, resentment, anger, and fear can distort our understanding. Such negative emotions can eat away at our objectivity; our fear can take away our ability to analyze a problem effectively. The resolution is to be utterly honest with ourselves, to be clear what our values are, and to recognize the extent to which our behavior patterns at times of stress divert us from the values that are most important to us. Having self-awareness about our emotions can help us keep the levelheadedness that can so easily disappear.

Self-awareness is not about self-indulgence; it is maintaining an honest appreciation of who we are, what our strengths are, and what our foibles are. A keen assessment of our own strengths and weaknesses is a precious gift. We all distort reality to some extent. Being self-aware enough to know when we distort reality in a way that can damage ourselves or others is very valuable.

In my book *Raise Your Game: How to Succeed at Work*, I suggest that a consistent message in challenging times is to be optimistic, energetic, and enthusiastic, while being rooted in realism. Being confident and building on your strengths can lead to a self-fulfilling prophecy of making the progress you desire. Success often flows from self-assuredness, because of the significant impact it has on enhancing capability. Drawing on your strengths means that even in the most challenging circumstances you can see opportunities. It enables you to believe that there is a solution, however tough the situation might seem.

Building on your strengths means being positive and objective. Optimism must not come across as denial. People who lose heart are those who have lost their positive belief that there can be a successful outcome. You have to believe that your strengths will mean that you can become part of the future and are not part of the problem. Growing your strengths can give you confidence that you can make choices, even in the most difficult of circumstances.

In Christian thinking there is sometimes the belief that since we are frail children of dust it is presumptuous to say we have strengths. But God has given us strengths to use. It is right that we show humility and are not cocky in the use of our strengths. But not using the gifts God has given us is an abdication of responsibility. So being self-aware about our strengths is a perfectly sensible starting point for prayerful decisions about next steps.

In their excellent book, *Now, Discover Your Strengths*, Marcus Buckingham and Donald Clifton talk about each individual needing to become an expert at finding, describing, applying, practicing, and refining his or her strengths. They distinguish natural talents from things you can learn; and they see strengths as a combination of talents, knowledge, and skills. Buckingham and Clifton encourage their readers to identify their five strongest themes of talent, some of which may not be strengths as of yet. Their thirty-four StrengthsFinder themes are set out in figure 3.

Figure 3

THE 34 THEMES OF STRENGTHSFINDER®

Achiever	Futuristic
Activator	Harmony
Adaptability	Ideation
Analytical	Includer
Arranger	Individualization
Belief	Input
Command	Intellection
Communication	Learner
Competition	Maximizer
Connectedness	Positivity
Consistency	Relator
Context	Responsibility
Deliberative	Restorative
Developer	Self-assurance
Discipline	Significance
Empathy	Strategic
Focus	Woo

StrengthsFinder® Profile[10]

Christians are often much better at articulating their vulnerabilities than their strengths. To an extent this is helpful, as being unaware of your vulnerabilities is a dangerous place to be. But being too bogged down in one's vulnerabilities can mean indecision and depression.

---

10.   Marcus Buckingham and Donald Clifton, *Now, Discover Your Strengths* (New York: Pocket Books, 2004), 73.

In *Raise Your Game: How to Succeed at Work*, I suggest that vulnerability can be dealt with using the following approach:

- Have self-awareness about the issue.
- Declare what has worked in the past to help reduce the issue.
- Believe there is evidence that the issue can be overcome.
- Adopt a focused approach that enables effective progress to be made.
- Declare that it is not an issue that is going to "get in the way" in the long run.

For Christians, there are additional factors:

- We can seek God's forgiveness for when our vulnerabilities caused problems in the past, and we will receive forgiveness when we genuinely seek it.
- We have the support and encouragement of others within the Christian communities of which we are a part.
- We have the example of the way Jesus encouraged and worked with those who felt vulnerable.
- We know that we are upheld by the love of God and that the Holy Spirit works within us.

Self-awareness can be about bringing before God all our strengths and vulnerabilities. It is about finding a sense of contentment as we lay before God all that we are. It is as we recognize and accept the human being God has created and acknowledge that we can become more whole and more complete in God's sight that we become fully comfortable with ourselves as a child of God. It is only as we accept our vulnerabilities that we can move on and build a greater coherence and equilibrium into our lives.

BEING AS SHREWD AS SNAKES
AND AS INNOCENT AS DOVES

Jesus encouraged his disciples to be "as shrewd as snakes and as innocent as doves" (Matthew 10:16). While I was at a theater in London recently, C. S. Lewis peered down from a great height and looked me firmly in the eye! The setting was a production of *Shadowlands*, which is about the marriage of Lewis and Joy Davidman. The play was about to begin, and Charles Dance, the actor playing Lewis, had walked on stage. The mobile phone belonging to the person next to me went off—but Charles Dance frowned severely at *me*, perhaps because I was in a suit and looked like a prime suspect! I tried to look "as innocent as a dove," but on this occasion my innocence did not appear to cut it.

In *Mere Christianity*, C. S. Lewis reflects on the words of Jesus about being as wise as serpents and as innocent, or harmless, as doves:

> Christ never meant that we were to remain children in *intelligence*: on the contrary. He told us to be not only "as harmless as doves," but also "as wise as serpents." He wants a child's heart, but a grown-up's head. He wants us to be simple, single-minded, affectionate, and teachable, as good children are; but He also wants every bit of intelligence we have to be alert at its job, and in first-class fighting trim. . . . The fact that what you are thinking about is God Himself (for example, when you are praying) does not mean that you can be content with the same babyish ideas which you had when you were a five-year-old.[11]

Lewis challenged his readers to hold that balance of a child's heart and a grown-up's head: the balance of being simple, single minded, and affectionate alongside using every bit of intelligence that is available to us.

---

11.   C. S. Lewis, *Mere Christianity* (New York: HarperCollins, 2001), 77.

What is the context for Matthew 10:16? Chapter 10 is the turning point in Matthew's Gospel. The first nine chapters have been full of wonderful teaching. The readers have learned of John's baptism and Jesus' baptism. We have heard the Sermon on the Mount, observed the faith of the centurion, and envisioned Jesus calming the storm and healing the multitudes. But now we move into a new act in the drama. It is time for the disciples to be sent out.

The initial phase of listening and observing moves into the disciples being given responsibility to "go out." As they go, they are to proclaim this message: "The kingdom of heaven has come near" (Matthew 10:7). Jesus said to them, "Freely you have received, freely give" (v. 8). They are told to greet people and bring peace; but where they are not welcomed, they are to shake the dust off their feet. Jesus cautioned them that he was sending them out like sheep among wolves and therefore advises them to be "as shrewd as snakes and as innocent as doves." So the context for the text is very clear: as the disciples set out into a potentially hostile world, they were to be as shrewd as snakes and as innocent as doves.

In his commentary on Matthew, Dick France wrote: "Christians are not to be gullible simpletons. But neither are they to be rogues. *Innocent* is literally 'unmixed,' i.e., pure, transparent; it demands not naivety, but an irreproachable honesty. The balance of prudence and purity will enable Christians both to survive and to fulfil their mission to the world."[12]

In *Matthew for Everyone*, Tom Wright included the following helpful paragraph about this text:

> Faced with this awesome challenge, Jesus' sharp advice to his
> followers was: be shrewd like snakes, but innocent like doves.
> Christians often find it easy to be one or the other, but seldom
> both. Without innocence, shrewdness becomes manipulative;
> without shrewdness, innocence becomes naivety. Though we

---

12. R. T. France, *Matthew* (Leicester, UK: Inter-Varsity, 1985), 182.

face different crises and different problems to those of the first disciples, we still need that finely balanced character, reflecting so remarkably that of Jesus himself. If we are in any way to face what he faced, and to share his work, we need to be sure that his own life becomes embodied in ours.[13]

Wright points to that finely balanced character of holding together wisdom and shrewdness alongside an innocence that is not naiveté. Shrewdness is being discerning, prudent, perceptive, and clearheaded. Innocence brings generosity of heart, compassion, understanding, listening, openness, and honesty. This phrase challenges us to think about the wisdom, shrewdness, and prudence that God has grown in us and how we might use those special gifts God has given us of listening, talking, writing, giving, and loving. Through continuous learning, giving, and serving, we can explore how God might grow, challenge, and cherish those gifts in us. It is not just about bringing wisdom; it is bringing innocence too. It means bringing an innocence that is open to fresh experiences of God's grace, open to new conversations, new insights, and new people so that we are receptive to new freshness and vitality in our pilgrimage of faith and life.

CONCLUSION

In this first section we have looked at what it means for the Christian leader to be rooted. We have talked about being rooted in God's created order; embedding the life of Jesus, the Christian themes, and the fruit of the Spirit; understanding human nature; growing in self-awareness; and being as shrewd as a snake and as innocent as a dove. Some final reflections:

- Allow yourself to enjoy the richness of God's created order

---

13. Tom Wright, *Matthew for Everyone: Part 1: Chapters 1–15* (London: SPCK Publishing, 2002), 117.

and the inspiration that comes from revisiting the life and work of Jesus.

- Keep believing that the Christian themes are a powerful influence for good in the world.
- Accept that embedding the fruit of the Spirit comes one step at a time.
- Be honest about your understanding of human nature and your own self-awareness.
- Allow yourself to be intuitive in recognizing human nature in others, bringing practical insight.
- Bring that combination of being as shrewd as a snake and as innocent as a dove in a way that brings enlightenment rather than destruction.

RADICAL

Jesus was a radical leader. Our calling needs to be radical too. Many leaders over the centuries have brought a strong sense of Christian values, which gave them the courage to think and act radically. Jesus kept taking people out of their comfort zones and encouraging them to be courageous. In this section we will look at the Christian's role in bringing an open mind and a challenging perspective. The section covers living with economic and global change, building vision and values in organizations, making hard decisions well, applying Christian principles at work, being an effective part of a team, and being clear about your profile as a Christian at work. It also covers working effectively with those of other faiths and being "salt and light" at work.

WHY SHOULD A CHRISTIAN BE RADICAL?

Jesus encouraged his followers to think in new and different ways. He took his disciples from the safety of the jobs they knew well into a very different form of lifestyle. He taught, stretched, and encouraged them. Following Jesus meant they were pushed in new and different directions and took on leadership roles that they had not previously anticipated. If the first disciples were willing to take radical steps, perhaps we should too.

WHO ARE YOUR ROLE MODELS?

Effective role models can be figures from history or individuals with whom we have particular associations now. There is a rich heritage of Christians who have done radical things. These have included Christian leaders who have addressed poverty; Christians in medical science who have initiated developments affecting the health of millions; Christians in education leadership who have ensured that students in their care have grown in mind, body, and spirit; and Christian visionaries who have led developments like the fair-trade movement and human relief organizations.

One example of a Christian leader who had a profound effect on society is William Wilberforce. The end of the eighteenth century was full of incidents that with the benefit of hindsight seem absurd. William Wilberforce faced an uphill battle to achieve the abolition of the slave trade.

What actions did the so-called civilized West condone? Let me take you to a ship captained by Luke Collingwood. The ship was full of slaves, many of whom were ill. Collingwood calculated that if the slaves died a natural death it would be a loss to the owners of the ship, but if they were thrown alive into the sea, it would be a loss to the underwriters. So 130 African slaves were thrown overboard, successfully disposing of the "cargo." When the event came to trial, the question was not about murder but about an insurance dispute regarding whether or not the insurers were obliged to pay for the loss of revenue.

One day a woman with a child in her arms was brought to be sold as a slave. The captain, Luke Collingwood, refused to buy her, not wishing to have a child on board. The trader brought her, looking sad and with no child, back the following day. Her child having been killed, the woman was now purchased by the captain.

Picture slave ships with the slaves shackled together by chains, thumbscrews used on those who misbehaved, and forceps employed to push food into the mouths of the uncooperative. Because sugar was profitable and slaves were cheap, plantation owners calculated that it was cheaper to flog half-a-dozen years' work out of a malnourished slave and buy another when that slave died than to provide good enough food and shelter to keep slaves alive longer. The squalor and brutality of their conditions were such that the life expectancy of a slave following captivity was only seven years.

Yet the British establishment and many God-fearing Christians turned a blind eye to slavery. It took a group of individuals who were ridiculed for their radicalism to change attitudes and bring about the end of the slave trade. At the center was Wilberforce. Though Wilberforce was only five feet tall and a mere seventy-six pounds, James Boswell wrote, "I saw what seemed a mere shrimp mount upon the table but as I listened he grew and grew and grew until the shrimp became a whale."

After Wilberforce became a Christian, he wrote to friends that he was not turning enthusiast and did not consider religion to necessitate being gloomy. He saw his faith as placing responsibility on every believer to be busy making the world a better place. He abhorred "shapeless idleness." In a letter to his sister, he assured her that he was not turning into a religious maniac but merely obeying the Bible, not becoming a hermit but being more "diligent in the business of life" than ever.

Being diligent in the business of life as a Christian set Wilberforce on a campaign trail to abolish the slave trade. In 1789 he introduced to Parliament his first bill to abolish the slave trade. Over the next decade bill after bill was blocked. The arguments against them now seem ridiculous:

- The slave trade was vital to the economy, their lordships warned each other.
- Hampering it would merely hand British trade to the French and would encourage slaves to revolt and massacre their masters.
- The Africans would be killed by their own enemies were

it not for the merciful alternative of transportation to the Caribbean.

- The lives of countless British families would be ruined if there was misplaced sensitivity toward Africans.
- The economy of Liverpool would collapse and people would be reduced to poverty because of the abolition of the slave trade.
- Wilberforce's campaign was religious and political fanaticism; if the bill was passed, no property could be reckoned as safe.

John Wesley's last written words were in the context of a letter addressed to Wilberforce: "If God be for you, who can be against you, so be not weary of well-doing. Go on in the name of God and in the power of his might till even American slavery (the vilest that ever saw the sun) shall vanish away before it."

Wilberforce used economic and theological arguments—economic in the sense that plantation owners had nothing to fear from abolition, theological through his repetition that he could not believe that the same God who forbids wanton bloodshed has made such violence necessary to the well-being of any part of his universe.[1]

Clearly Wilberforce was a Christian who was "diligent in the business of life." He possessed *passion* to abolish inhuman inactivity, *persistence* to introduce one bill after another and to commit his resources of both time and money to the cause, and *patience* to be unrelenting in building alliances.

Wilberforce was part of the Clapham Sect, a group of Christians in public life who encouraged and helped each other to grow in resolve to live out their faith in a practical way and thus make a massive difference

---

1.   To learn more about William Wilberforce, I recommend Stephen Tomkins, *William Wilberforce: A Biography* (Oxford: Lion Hudson, 2007).

in society. There was a famous tree near Croydon where Wilberforce and William Pitt, the future prime minister, met and resolved that the slave trade should be brought to an end. In 1982 the tree died, and now just a stump remains. The site is overgrown and surrounded by barbed wire. A new sapling was planted, but it is still overshadowed by the carcass of the ancient oak. Some have suggested that this might be a metaphor for the modern-day church's reluctance to engage with issues of social justice.

The society that Wilberforce addressed was enslaved to inherited attitudes that needed to be broken. Slaves were seen as goods to be bought and sold. Humanity and compassion had no place. William Wilberforce was God's agent—diligent in the business of life—who, through his passion, persistence, and patience, provides a fascinating role model for us a mere two hundred years later.

William Wilberforce is only one of many Christian leaders throughout history who have exemplified passion, persistence, and patience. Leaders like Wilberforce, the first Earl of Shaftesbury, Mother Teresa, and others have brought clarity of faith, a determination to make a difference, and a willingness to go against social norms and expectations. They were all "diligent in the business of life"—ready to speak out against contemporary attitudes and behaviors.

Questions to consider might be:
- Does a leader like William Wilberforce, with his single-minded determination, inspire you or make you recoil?
- How willing are you to go against the socially accepted norms of the day and speak of the need for radical change?
- How relevant to you are Wilberforce's words about being "diligent in the business of life"?

In addition to leaders from history, our role models include experienced leaders today. When I asked a number of people what characteristics of Christian leaders in the global workplace most inspire them, the following were some of their responses:

- "John was always inspiring because he was open about his mistakes. He could be macho and traditional, but there was a freshness about his faith and work/life balance. He wanted to give time to people. He was a good man without being dogmatic."
- "Mary clearly gains energy from her faith. She doesn't worry like the rest of us. She has a profound belief that whatever the situation things will work out for good. She holds her nerve and exudes a calmness."
- "Chiang was always willing to support others. He brought a strong sense of servant leadership that inspired people to become more adventurous and bold in what they said and did."
- "Bill, one of the senior executives in the bank, went on a personal retreat each year; it clearly helped him to get the wider issues into perspective and meant there was a measuredness in his approach."
- "Hazel always brought tough realism. On the one hand she seemed to have a very hard attitude, but her Christian faith showed in her consistency, thoroughness, and fairness."
- "Richard was an extraordinary leader who brought forgiveness, authenticity, humility, and vision. He lived the values that are most important to him and it showed through."
- "Henry was inspirational. He was always authentic and transparent, bringing wisdom and commitment."

What is particularly interesting about these reflections is that they are of leaders who were often hard rather than soft, open rather than closed, active rather than passive, and engaged rather than just observing. Some of the key themes relate to transparency, openness, commitment, wisdom, and authenticity. Of course, gentleness, compassion, and kindness are important. But often what people particularly remember and respect about Christians in leadership roles is their ability to be clear and tough when necessary.

Key questions to ask yourself might be:

- Who are the role models who have most inspired you in a work context? What characteristics of these leaders have had the biggest impact upon you?
- What are the key features of Christian leaders who have had the biggest impact on you?
- How important are the themes of consistency and authenticity in Christian role models at work?
- Where do you think your role models have gotten it right or wrong on the balance between the tougher and the gentler aspects of leadership?

WHAT MIGHT BEING RADICAL MEAN?

Being radical is not about being obnoxious or different just for the sake of being obnoxious or different. It is recognizing that there is often a tendency toward inaction or complacency. The Christian can build on objectivity that is distinctive through not being wedded to a particular organizational way of doing things. Since Christians believe that their integrity before God comes first, they may be less swayed by the moods of the economic cycle or the views of the current leaders.

Just as Jesus was radical, Christian leaders can have the scope to be radical in the way they contribute to how organizations live with economic and global change, respond to the leadership attributes needed in the future, and build and live out vision and values in organizations.

LIVING WITH RAPID ECONOMIC
AND GLOBAL CHANGE

Sometimes change is imperceptible; at other times it is dramatic. It is only when we look back that we see the full effect of changes affecting our society and economy. In recent years there have been profound changes in the availability of information, the speed with which transactions can be made, the amount of available data, and the speed of communications. Information and activity have never been more intense. There are hugely positive benefits in terms of availability of information, a greater understanding of the reasons for particular events, increased accessibility to health care and education, and a greater voice being given to the customer.

And yet many of the changes have not been for the better. Poverty, crime, violence, and the breakup of family relationships have become ever more acute. Progress often seems short lived. We put a great deal of effort into building the transformation in particular areas, only to see progress dissipate when the focus of the day moves on to another priority area. Those who live most effectively with economic and social change appear to bring a clarity about values that are most important to them and an ability to keep their nerve during times of acute turbulence.

Good leaders know how to manage periods of change, but what happens when that change is sustained and driven by forces outside their control and when its scale of pace is unprecedented? Sudden changes in business fortunes combined with high levels of uncertainty and rumor are extremely difficult to manage. The coaching partnership of which I am a member, Praesta Partners, did some action research in 2008 with leaders in different sectors who had been through times of extended turbulence. We asked them what they had learned from their experiences. What are the fundamentals that matter? What can leaders do to ensure that they continue to perform at their best?

What came out of this research was the consistent message that the characteristics identified as important in turbulent times are the leadership fundamentals. During turbulent times, strong leaders

- maintain their core values and beliefs, no matter how much pressure they come under;
- tackle each new challenge clearly and calmly, leading from the front to inspire those around them; and
- know how to care for themselves in order to maintain stamina and well-being, often for a lengthy and exhausting period.

Maintain Core Values and Beliefs

In regard to maintaining core attitudes and beliefs, a common theme was that focusing on what you believe to be "the right thing to do" gives a sense of personal integrity, self-worth, and even accomplishment—no matter what the final outcome. What you consider to be right can come from your own values and experiences or from having considered the perspective of trusted advisers.

We repeatedly heard about the immense effort needed to keep doing what you believe is right when under intense pressure. It can be tempting to go for quick wins, make a small compromise, or focus on the most attractive numbers just to make others feel better or to make yourself look good; but the consequence is that you inadvertently begin to lose your way. The forces pulling at you can help clarify what you really believe. We sometimes truly discover what we believe to be right only when pushed to make very difficult decisions.

The research demonstrated the importance of being honest with yourself during challenging times. This includes focusing your time and energy and recognizing when you may be on the verge of "losing it." Many leaders describe the feelings of pressure that they have to do it all, that they should have all the answers and be able to solve everything on their own. In challenging times, effective leaders will know what they do well and accept the limits of their abilities. They will concentrate on what they alone can uniquely do and delegate the rest.

Leaders talk of feeling disappointed, resentful, exhausted, angry, or afraid during turbulent times. These are powerful emotions that can fundamentally affect our ability to view things logically or to act rationally. The lesson is that when leaders sense themselves closing down, lacking in confidence, blaming others, or not listening, they should acknowledge their problem and be honest with themselves regarding whether they are in danger of becoming emotionally overwhelmed. They need to be clear how their reaction might be affecting their work and the people around them and then be willing to step away and take a break, however brief, from the situation.

Cultivating a positive mindset was seen to be important during challenging times. This means believing that no matter how intractable the challenge may appear there is a way out of it. This means focusing on what can be done, not on what has gone wrong, and bringing "grounded optimism" rather than "false optimism." Grounded optimism requires a constructive mindset combined with a healthy realism about what is going on.

Tackle Each New Challenge Clearly and Calmly

The evidence from our research suggested that, when faced with day-to-day decisions and issues during turbulence, the most effective leaders continue to find their role and their success within the context of the bigger picture. They have a sense of who they are and what they stand for, which goes beyond their current job. Therefore they resist being subsumed by any specific situation or crisis. They do this by focusing on four things: keeping a sense of perspective, setting priorities, having the right people around them, and leading visibly from the front.

The temptation to lose perspective is one of the first things leaders have experienced during challenging, unpredictable times. This can involve being unable to put each issue or decision in context, understand how real of a threat it represents, assess the scale of its impact, or decide if it has long-term implications. Under pressure, it is easy to feel drawn to action, and the normal "thinking time" can seem like a luxury. However counterintuitive it might seem, a crucial lesson of turbulent times is the need to step back and to think, even for a short time. Leaders stressed the need to stay focused during turbulent times and identified four fundamental ways of informing their decisions: getting the best data possible, listening to others' views, having personal sounding boards, and creating personal space.

Setting clear priorities is particularly difficult when the day-to-day reality is constantly changing and unpredictable. It is easy to get sucked into becoming a "firefighter" and lurching from one crisis to another. The most effective leaders during turbulence are as clear as possible with themselves and others about where they want to take the organization and what everyone needs to do to get there. At the same time, they have the flexibility to adapt quickly when circumstances or perspectives change in the light of new information. The key is to keep their nerve in the face of panic or pressure from others—having the courage to do what will make the biggest difference in terms of long-term success, sometimes choosing between a set of equally unattractive options.

During extreme challenge a team needs to be highly performing with the right people in the right roles. The team needs to be loyal, committed, aligned, and collaborative. It is crucial to be surrounded by people who are both on your side and able to openly disagree during debates before reaching agreement about what to do. When pressure and uncertainty reveals flaws and gaps in experience in a team, leaders need to ensure the necesary changes are made as quickly as possible. There is often not the luxury of waiting to see. Our research showed that making changes in a team, even if painful, was often essential in order for progress to be made. Pulling together under real pressure can result in amazing creativity and output. Pressure on a group to think the unthinkable can force creativity and ideas.

In times of uncertainty, stress, and panic, people need to see a leader who is calm, focused, and inspiring. The evidence from our research reinforced the importance of visible, personal leadership keeping everyone informed and publicly setting the tone for how the whole organization is expected to react and behave.

During extreme uncertainty it is unlikely that you will have many answers to people's questions. However, experience has shown the danger of going silent within the organization and spending too much time in a huddle with your immediate team. Silence breeds rumor and negativity. People need information to be able to understand where to focus their priorities and how to offer ideas.

People will not only be listening to your words but also be observing your body language, facial expressions, and tone of voice. People will look for any signals that you feel things are out of control. The perception of the leader's mood will spread like wildfire and will often become distorted through gossip. Many refer to the "cheerleader" element of a leader's role in turbulent times, a role that may require putting on a leadership mask.

Look After Your Well-Being

Leading an organization and its people through radical changes and pressures requires a high level of stamina and personal strength. For many leaders, focusing on one's own well-being can seem like self-indulgence. They explain that it can feel as if every moment matters and that it is important to dig in and work all the hours they can in order to ensure that the organization and its people are on track. While this may work in a short-term crisis, if you don't take care of yourself over the longer term, the danger is that you can lose perspective and the energy to make tough decisions.

There is growing evidence that looking after ourselves fundamentally affects our ability to be at our best. Rather than something optional, this is foundational for leadership success. Being in good shape will mean having the inner resources to dig deep into your energy and resilience and not let the tank run dry.

The evidence from our research, as well as from many commentators, indicates that there are four central areas of well-being. In *Riding the Rapids*, Jane Stephens and I suggested that leaders should assess themselves in the following four areas:

- **Physical well-being.** Building stamina fuels creative and mental energy. This involves a combination of physical exercise and relaxation time. One CEO explained the impact of improving his health: "A few years ago I was heavier than I am today. Losing weight has helped me cope with difficult situations. I am totally clear that mental capacity is affected by physical capacity."
- **Emotional well-being.** Finding a state of equilibrium helps you remain calm and balanced. For some this is supported by their relationships, for others by confidence in their sense of self-worth and unique value.
- **Intellectual well-being.** Engaging your mind in something other than everyday work, no matter how trivial, can be a source of relief and can stimulate creativity.
- **Spiritual well-being.** Knowing what matters most in your life keeps things in perspective—whether it comes from enduring interests or relationships or is rooted in beliefs and faith.

Riding the Rapids was written for leaders in the secular world who have a variety of different leadership perspectives. Readers have responded positively to the ideas in the booklet, including the four strands of well-being. Those who may not come with a faith perspective are often still happy to reflect on spiritual well-being as well as physical, emotional, and intellectual well-being. This can provide the opportunity for those whose spiritual well-being comes from belief or faith to share their perspective and to dialogue in an open and honest way with leaders who come from a different perspective.

Jane Stephens and I concluded that being a leader in turbulent times in the global workplace is tough and exhausting. Leaders have to learn to live with a higher level of challenge, pressure, and stress as a normal part of working life rather than just a short-term crisis. This requires resilience, stamina, and focus. Leaders who are physically and mentally strong are able to accept change, learn from it, and even thrive under pressure. They regard a challenge as an opportunity, a chance to learn and to deepen their experience. Their ability to be flexible, positive, and energetic comes to the fore and separates them from other leaders. A crucial step is taking back control of your life, whatever the external pressures upon you.

What does being radical mean for a Christian in a leadership role at a time of rapid change? It means maintaining core values, tackling each challenge calmly, and looking after your physical, emotional, mental, and spiritual welfare. It means being fully present when handling difficult situations but not being fully absorbed in the day-to-day pressures. It means enabling the rootedness of your Christian faith to give you both a secure perspective about what is important and a willingness to bring fresh new approaches to address difficult issues.

IMPORTANT LEADERSHIP ATTRIBUTES IN THE FUTURE

I asked a range of leaders about the leadership attributes that will matter most in the future. Figure 4 sets out some of their comments.

Figure 4

IMPORTANT LEADERSHIP
ATTRIBUTES IN THE FUTURE

"More and more, leaders need to understand people in a far more coherent way, be it employees or customers. It is crucial to understand people's behaviors. The ability to communicate will be vital in a world where perception can play a crucial role. You need to understand the modern world. Running a team is very different now than ten years ago. Increasingly, more will depend on the digital media. By applying the core values of being a Christian you will always provide a sound framework."—*private sector leader*

"Emotional intelligence and relationships are very important. It is all about getting relationships right—getting people on the bus; then it is about being able to move quickly and think quickly."—*chief executive*

"Emotional intelligence—the ability to work in a global sense. I am not a great fan of virtual leadership, but it is going to become increasingly important."—*private sector leader*

"The importance of integrity and honesty. Integrity needs to be reestablished. What is so important is the way we convey decisions to people. Jesus translated the complex into simple terms. The ability to communicate is so important. Decisions should always be seen to be based on integrity. There is so much cynicism in the world."—*political leader*

"Self-honesty, a sense of duty, and responsibility for your actions. Being responsible, linked with the importance of sharing the risks. Not asking people to do what you would not do yourself. Carrying a sense of personal integrity. Having the courage of your convictions. Having the confidence to be clear about what you are doing with your life. Being fair and being seen to be fair when making decisions. Seeking to do what is right."—*human resources director*

"I am very concerned about exhaustion, stress, and depression because of a 24/7 world. Leadership tends to have a cult of personalities. There is a danger of people claiming that wisdom is their idea when they have taken it on from others."—*local government leader*

"There needs to an adaptive leadership style that enables you to respond and cope. Authentic leadership is important. It is seeing things through and coping with the relentless spotlight of the media. How you make the journey and are seen to make the journey is important."—*finance director*

"The key to leadership in the future is how you lead people. In an IT world, what will matter is more awareness about cultural background and respecting people's values in an environment where you understand the people-impact and how best to build relationships. There is a growing problem of facelessness in a mass-communication world. There is a breakdown of personal relationships and communication. Communication takes place so often now through IT rather than through people. But the theme of the quality of the relationship is crucial to success."—*private sector leader*

"Servant leadership will continue to be important, but you must be careful in using it. You have to be good at what you do. Being first class as a professional in the field is important. You have to bring a clarity of thinking. There has to be professionalism, integrity, and servant leadership."—*senior international banker*

"What is going to matter are transparency and honesty. It is just as important in commerce as in the public sector. There are examples of turning a blind eye. What is necessary is that the company thinks it is important to maintain integrity or it will cost them something. It is important to empower the right people. You need to empower them with ethical standards."—*senior international banker*

"Being clear what your values are in a world that is full of egos."
—*university leader*

"Attributes that will matter most will be the same for Christians and non-Christians. It is about winning the hearts and minds of people to achieve common objectives. To develop a vision and communicate is important whether or not you are a Christian. How you inspire is crucial. Emotional intelligence is always important. The actions we take must always be done with integrity."—*chief executive*

Key themes that are central to these comments are the importance of integrity and values, the quality of relationships, the ability to communicate and cope with the speed of communications, and the capacity to work effectively in a more virtual way.

My own view is that the key attributes of leaders over the next few years will need to include

- rootedness in values and the ability to communicate those values and the resulting behaviors clearly;
- a quality of analysis that will draw from a range of different perspectives and professional input;
- a combination of authenticity and adaptability whereby the leader comes across as consistent in his or her values while adaptable in finding solutions that meet a particular context;
- an ability to make decisions quickly while building as much agreement as possible;
- the capacity to bring out the best in others, developing their confidence and self-reliance; and
- a willingness to find the balance between focused work and being immersed in other activities that give you vitality.

Key questions to ask yourself about leadership attributes in light of economic and global change might include:

- What have you noticed that is different in leaders who are successful now compared to twenty years ago?
- What economic and global changes do you think affect you as a leader most significantly?
- What leadership challenges are the current pace of change putting into sharp focus for you?
- What helps you keep your focus and equilibrium during challenging times?

BUILDING VISION AND VALUES IN ORGANIZATIONS

Many organizations have statements of vision and values. Sometimes we can be tempted to be cynical about such statements or phrases. We think that an organization having a "mission" statement is somehow pinching a word from a Christian context and subverting the use of that word by applying it in a secular context. But an organization deciding to have a clear "mission" or "vision" is not secularizing a Christian concept; it is recognizing the importance of organizations having a clarity of objective and aspiration.

Looking after our values is both a personal responsibility and a corporate responsibility. When an organization has a set of values, there is a responsibility for individuals to both live those values and encourage others to do the same. The best organizations have a clear articulation of their vision and values and what it means for different people. This provides an effective benchmark against which individuals can assess what behaviors are appropriate and what the consequence of living those values will be.

A good example of an articulation of vision and values and what it means for staff, customers, and delivery partners was published in 2007 by the UK Department for Communities and Local Government (fig. 5). It provides a clear framework for making decisions. Another excellent example is the recently adopted mission, values, and delivery outcomes of the West Mercia Police Constabulary (fig. 6), in which case the use of the word "I" puts a strong focus on individuals living the values.

A corporate vision and values statement can be a powerful tool *or* irrelevant. When they are thought through well, they can provide a framework within which the Christian can live and work effectively.

In *Change: How to Adapt and Transform the Business,* N. Anand describes a corporate vision as

> an idea of the future that acts as a focal point for all change efforts. Vision is about having a picture of the changed organisation as it will be when change has been successful: A sense of "how it looks when it works." To be an effective tool, vision has to have substance. It should not be a management fantasy, slogan or platitude. Good visions function as useful guides and inspiration to those who have to make changes happen. They help to cut through doubts and details by getting to the heart of whether any particular project or action is the right one—does it contribute to realising our vision? If not, should it proceed?[2]

Anand emphasizes that a good vision is clear and intelligible to all those in the organization, giving them a common goal toward which to work. Just as the necessity for change needs to be articulated in a common language, a vision needs to express the desired future in a universally comprehensive way.

The management thinker John Kotter sees clear vision as a crucial part of ensuring effective change. His themes are to increase urgency,

---

2.   N. Anand, ed., *Change: How to Adapt and Transform the Business* (Norwich, UK: Format, 2004).

Figure 5

UK GOVERNMENT DEPARTMENT: DEPARTMENT FOR COMMUNITIES AND LOCAL GOVERNMENT

OUR VISION

Creating great places where people want to live, work and raise a family

OUR VALUES

We are ambitious and creative.	We act openly and as one department.	We give people the chance to shine.	We give people a voice.

What it means for our staff

We focus on delivering effectively, stretching ourselves, exceeding people's expectations and always looking for ways to lift our game.	We work well together. Our communications and actions are open, honest and straightforward, and we listen to what others have to say.	We respect and value individuals, unlock and develop their talents, give them the opportunity to grow, take responsibility and celebrate and reward their contributions.	We welcome questions and ideas, and we respect everyone's contributions. We challenge and respond well to challenge.

What it means for people and communities

Improving places and communities, using money wisely and where it can make the greatest difference.	We welcome people's views and work with them to make communities stronger and more cohesive.	Individuals and communities are treated with respect and are given opportunities to contribute to our work.	We empower people and communities to speak out and shape their neighbourhoods.

What it means for delivery partners

We forge strong partnerships built on a shared vision and what works best in practice.	We work with partners so that together we deliver the greatest possible benefits. Our partners can trust what we say and do.	We respect and value everyone we work with. We give partners the chance to show the best that they can do—for those we all serve.	We give responsibility for delivery to those best able to make the biggest difference.

build the guiding team, get the vision right, communicate for buy-in, empower action, create short-term wins, don't let up, and make change stick through striving for sustainability. In communicating a vision of

Figure 6

WEST MERCIA POLICE		
OUR MISSION		
Serving–Protecting–Making the Difference		
OUR VALUES		
I act with honesty, fairness and respect in serving our communities and the people within them.	I take pride in working within an organisation dedicated to protecting people and upholding the law.	I always take responsibility; my contribution makes a valued difference.
Successful delivery of our mission between now and 2012 will result in the following outcomes:		
The public have confidence in us and express satisfaction with our policing service.	Levels of crime and anti-social behaviour remain low.	Our communities feel safe.

change, Kotter encourages leaders to keep it simple, repeat and reinforce the message, don't act in a way that is inconsistent with the vision, address any perceived inconsistencies between vision and action, and make communication two way.[3]

These insights are relevant whether we are helping to create a vision for an organization, moving forward a corporate vision within our part of the organization, or interrelating a corporate and personal vision so that we are able to contribute within an organization with energy and integrity.

An important area is the interplay between individual and corporate values. The interplay should be a two-way process. If values are going to have any impact in an organization, there must be an opportunity for people working in the organization to influence the creation and living

---

3.   John P. Kotter, *Leading Change: Why Transformation Efforts Fail* (Boston: Harvard Business Press, 1996).

out of those values. If they are presented in a top-down way, they will rapidly be ignored. If the consultation is vague and woolly, resulting in no clear and concise values, then the whole process will be regarded as a waste of time. If the resulting values are wordy or perceived to be fudged, they will have no impact.

The senior team needs to define the final values in such a way that there is simplicity and clarity, with individuals seeing consistency between personal and organizational values. Though the senior team needs to demonstrate that a listening process has been going on, at the end of the day it is the team's job to set clear and concise values. Values will be at their most powerful when there is a synergy between personal and organizational components.

In 2002 the board of the Department for Education and Skills, of which I was a member, went through a significant process. After an extensive consultation period, the board defined the following behaviors as the center point of the change it wanted to encourage:

- We are determined to make a difference.
- We listen and value diversity.
- We are honest and open.
- We innovate and challenge.
- We learn and improve.

The initial draft had been modified as a result of focus groups across the organization, in which the plea was for simplicity and clarity. Each of us who were members of the departmental board tried to build the behaviors into the organization by living them out, constantly referring to them and ensuring that they were fully reflected in performance assessments. We recognized that the behaviors often needed to be linked together when an individual was deciding on a particular course of action. We also recognized that there could well be a tension between "We listen and value diversity" and "We are determined to make a difference." The challenge of living the behaviors was to reconcile these values in an open and frank way in order to reach the most appropriate conclusions.

The board was very conscious that there needed to be a unity between personal and organizational values. As board members, we needed to demonstrate these behaviors, or else the rest of the organization would not take them seriously. We openly asked to be challenged about whether the values were being lived. The fact that the behaviors were fully embedded meant that when there were major controversial issues there was a clear touchstone on which to base our reactions and assess how well we had done.

The behaviors that we adopted as the board of the Department for Education and Skills worked because of the consultation, the clarity about the behaviors, and the fact that we were continually testing whether we were living by them. I still carry that list of behaviors in the top pocket of my suit jacket.

The more an organization focuses on vision and values, the more it provides both an opportunity and a responsibility for Christians to express their views. Trying to influence an organization's vision or values is not about a blinkered attempt to force your own views on others. It is about participating in responsible leadership where you can make a difference both in the way vision and values are put together and in how they are lived within an organization. Once an organization has defined its values, they become a benchmark whereby leaders will be assessed either formally through staff attitude surveys or informally as measured by the level of vitality and energy within the organization.

The growing attention being given to business ethics enables individuals to examine the interrelation between their personal values and those of the organization they work for in a more constructive way than was perhaps the case a few years ago. The high profile of the Institute of Business Ethics in the UK is evidence of this increased focus. In its publication, *Setting the Tone: Ethical Business Leadership*, Philippa Foster Back identifies some of the tensions that can exist between differing sources of values: society, through the legislative process; individuals, through their personal values; professional bodies and the norms they set; and companies, which lay down codes of ethics for their staff to follow.[4]

Foster Back suggests that the crucial challenge is building trust. She describes the five attributes of an ethical business leader as openness, fair-mindedness, honesty, courage, and the ability to listen. She describes the five key behaviors of such an ethical leader as

- being open-minded and cultivating themselves and others through a willingness to learn;
- being independent and willing to stand up and be counted, challenging the status quo;
- being aware and knowing that doing the right thing is the right thing to do;
- being considerate and cautious in managing expectations; and
- being determined and direct without fear of confrontation, actively stamping out poor behavior.[5]

Questions for reflection:
- How important is it to you to be regarded as an ethical business leader?
- How independent minded should you be? In what situations would you be willing to stand up and be counted?
- How do you balance being "determined and direct" with being "considerate and cautious"?
- How would you test whether your sense of "the right thing to do" is correct?

---

4.   Philippa Foster Back, *Setting the Tone: Ethical Business Leadership* (London: Institute of Business Ethics, 2005).
5.   Ibid.

Building vision and values into organizations can apply just as much to your part of the organization as well as to the organization overall. While the behaviors that are lived in your part of the organization need to be consistent with behaviors in the organization as a whole, there will be opportunities to ensure that the values that are most important to you and your team are reinforced.

Key questions to ask yourself might be:
- Is there more I could do to reinforce the focus on vision and values in the organization as a whole?
- What opportunities does the framework for vision and values in the organization provide to help me in the way I lead my part of the organization?

The challenge to the Christian is to play a full part in the way vision and values are developed and lived in an organization. Being radical may well be about being active in discussions that formulate and assess how a vision and values are working. It might be about quietly reinforcing behaviors that enable an organization to work with harmony and purpose.

MAKING HARD DECISIONS WELL

Tough decisions come in many different shapes and sizes. For any leader or manager, there are decisions covering strategic direction, resourcing, priorities, communications, and the management of staff. The Gospels record Jesus making many different types of decisions. He made hard decisions when he became an itinerant preacher, picked his disciples, chose who to disagree with and where to pitch the level of controversy, and determined to go to Jerusalem—despite the fact it would lead to Gethsemane, interrogation, and crucifixion. In my book *Deciding Well: A Christian Perspective on Making Decisions as a Leader*, I suggest that some of the features of Jesus' decision making were:
- **Boldness:** He was willing to set out a clear way forward even

if others did not agree. He was willing to take risks and to incur the skepticism or disagreement of others.

- **Commitment**: He stuck with his choice of disciples even though they exasperated him at times by their slowness of learning and lack of courage.
- **Resoluteness**: There was a resolve in the way he made decisions and stood by them. He set his face toward Jerusalem, knowing that it would lead to his crucifixion; but he remained undeterred from this intent.
- **Clarity**: Jesus did not hide who he was or the nature of his calling. He was unequivocal and consistent under questioning or interrogation, though sometimes who he was was only fully clear with the benefit of hindsight.

Some of the characteristics of the way Jesus handled hard decisions include the following: A clarity of purpose provided a framework for his hard decisions. He understood the wider context of state and church politics as he talked with leaders and understood where they were coming from. He retained his ability to be compassionate and express his humanity, even when he was making hard decisions. He sought opportunities to withdraw and reflect. He was willing to make the decisions only he could make, and he was prepared to live by those decisions. He prepared for hard decisions; for example, he spent the night in prayer prior to the selection of his key team of twelve disciples (Luke 6:12–16).

When Jesus made hard decisions, he drew on various forms of awareness. He embodied

- physical awareness, by being with people in close quarters;
- emotional awareness, by understanding people's needs, hopes, and fears;
- intellectual awareness, through his discussing and debating issues and his telling parables to stretch his hearers' thinking; and

- spiritual awareness, in terms of understanding people's deepest needs for forgiveness, new life, and hope.

Jesus had a remarkable ability to combine these four aspects of awareness when talking with individuals. For example, as he spoke with the Samaritan woman at the well (recorded in John 4), there was his physical presence, his awareness of her particular emotional needs, his discussion with her at an intellectual level about the significance of living water, and his spiritual awareness of her need to worship the Father in spirit and truth. Jesus was both the Son of God and a human leader. Thus, reflecting on his approach to decisions brings both an awareness of God's purposes expressed through Jesus as the Son of God and an awareness of the best of thoughtful human leadership.

Based on the experiences of Christians in a variety of leadership roles who were called upon to make hard decisions, *Deciding Well* draws out the best of experience first from the secular context and then from a Christian perspective. It identifies ten points of good practice in each area, as follows:

Developing Your Capacity to Make Hard Decisions:
General Understanding and Skills

1. **Observe others making decisions.** Watching those who make decisions well can be very revealing. After you have seen someone make a good decision with a constructive outcome, it may be worth writing down what he or she did well and sharing that perspective with a friend or colleague. In workshops, I often invite people to identify generic characteristics of good decision makers. It is equally helpful to look at bad decisions or decision makers and crystallize the learning about what has gone wrong. The important step is then applying this learning to the way *you* make decisions.

2. **Bring as much clarity as possible.** This is about training

yourself to be as objective as possible and being willing to base decisions on firm evidence, even when the evidence is contrary to what you had previously assumed. It means asking questions such as *What are the facts? Do I have the right information?* and *What are the risks?*

3. **Understand your convictions.** This has to do with understanding and applying your values, intuition, and trained judgment. It is recognizing that facts always have to be set in the wider context of values and beliefs. We need to develop an understanding about when our instinctive reaction is a reliable guide and when there is an emotional distortion embedded within it.

4. **Build up self-knowledge.** Good decision makers understand their own strengths and weaknesses and are not caught in a spiral of self-analysis. They know enough about themselves to interpret their own reactions and perspectives accurately. This self-knowledge can come through personal reflection, feedback from others, or psychometric assessments.

5. **Learn from experience.** Whether a decision has gone right or wrong, there is always a scope for learning. Stepping back to write down the three or four learning points when a decision has gone well or badly is never wasted. We can so easily move remorselessly from one decision to another without ever taking stock and reflecting. Looking at three or four learning points rather than twenty-five can help us focus on next steps instead of being daunted by an excessively long list.

6. **Be willing to make decisions.** So often we can be caught in indecision where we keep going through the arguments again and again. Often we have to decide on the basis of partial information. Avoiding making a decision is making a decision not to take an action! The learning comes from making the

decision, observing your own reaction and the responses of those around you, and then having the confidence to keep making decisions.

7. **Grow your courage.** Courage is the ability to step out into the unknown. Growing courage is not about becoming foolhardy; it is seeing opportunities, assessing risks, and being willing to take a consistent set of actions. Growing courage will involve both being aware of the perspective of others and sometimes developing a thicker skin, so that your courage is informed by but not quashed by the views of those around you.

8. **Develop your communication skills.** Becoming a better communicator as you make decisions starts from growing your listening, engaging, and persuading skills without falling into the trap of appearing to manipulate. It is watching your words and expressions. It is fine-tuning both the tone and the content. So often an individual can win an argument but leave the other person unpersuaded because his or her approach and demeanor have been dismissive.

9. **Build sounding boards.** Good decision makers have built a sequence of sounding boards with whom to test out their ideas, such as a trusted colleague at work, a mentor who has wide experience, or a coach who brings to bear perspectives from a wide variety of different worlds. Building a good sounding board is not ducking responsibility. Rather, it is recognizing that your responsibilities are such that it is vital to triangulate your perspective with others and to view issues from a variety of perspectives. Hence the value of building a network of personal support covering wise people from within and outside your particular sphere.

10. **Obtain feedback.** Quality feedback given in a positive and supportive way is one of the most valuable gifts an individual

can receive. This may be realized by seeking out individuals whom you trust and whom you can ask directly for feedback, using an independent person like a coach, or taking advantage of a 360-degree assessment instrument. It is important to interpret feedback with care; not all feedback is accurate, as it may be distorted by the perspective of the observer. What matters is consciously deciding how you are going to embed the learning from feedback.

Developing Your Capacity to Make Hard Decisions:
Christian Understanding and Skills

1. **Embed the life and teaching of Jesus.** The distinctiveness of the Christian perspective comes through embedding the life and teachings of Jesus. This will likely involve reading or listening to sections from the Gospels on a regular basis so that you are refreshed by the life, actions, and words of Jesus. This means being open to the continued relevance of Gospel stories. It may mean asking yourself, "What would Jesus do?" in particular circumstances and seeing whether posing that question helps clarify relevant principles. Paul wrote to the Colossians, "Just as you received Christ Jesus as Lord, continue to live your lives in him, rooted and built up in him" (Colossians 2:6–7). Walking in Christ, and aiming to embrace his approach through continually renewing our understanding of his life and teachings, is the foundation stone for bringing a Christian perspective to decision making.

2. **Reflect on Scripture.** Getting into the biblical narrative in the Old and New Testaments and visualizing being present when decisions were made can enable us to understand more readily why those decisions were made and to learn from the

experiences of the individuals involved. For example: Why did Abraham, Moses, Jonah, and Paul make the decisions they did, and how is that relevant to you? Reflecting on the Scriptures might mean absorbing the words of one chapter of the Book of Proverbs or one Psalm each day and letting its significance influence the decisions you make that day. It could mean reflecting on how the fruit of the Spirit, summarized by Paul as love, joy, peace, patience, kindness, goodness, faithfulness, gentleness, and self-control (Galatians 5:22–23), can influence the way we make decisions.

3. **Nurture wisdom.** The Old Testament includes a section called Wisdom Literature, which is full of practical advice. The psalmist exhorts, "Show me your ways, LORD, teach me your paths" (Psalm 25:4) and "He guides me along the right paths for his name's sake" (Psalm 23:3). Wisdom is seen as traveling along the right paths. J. I. Packer and Carolyn Nystrom suggest that "wisdom is indeed pragmatic . . . but it is humble, honest, realistic, insightful, generous, compassionate, stabilizing and encouraging also."[6] In the New Testament, James wrote, "If any of you lacks wisdom, you should ask God, who gives generously to all without finding fault, and it will be given to you" (James 1:5). Seeking and nurturing wisdom is an important part of developing the capacity to make good decisions.

4. **Learn from role models.** It can be helpful to consider decisions made by Christians both in earlier generations and in the current era, reflecting on what we can learn from them. William Wilberforce saw his calling as a Christian to be

---

6.   J. I. Packer and Carolyn Nystrom, *Guard Us, Guide Us: Divine Leading in Life's Decisions* (Grand Rapids: Baker, 2008), 112–137.

diligent in the business of life, hence his resolve to end the slave trade. Mother Teresa was determined to have a strong impact on reducing child poverty in India. Pioneers with a vision have brought focused energy to developing aid organizations. Learning from such leaders can provide a sense of inspiration when approaching decisions conscious of the long-term effect they can have on others. Reading biographies can provide a rich vein of inspiring stories.

5. **Recognize and use your gifts.** The gifts we have are not to be ignored. Can we allow ourselves to believe that God has given us gifts that exist in order to be used? This is not about being proud or arrogant about our gifts; it is about using them in a constructive way. Allowing ourselves to be encouraged by the gifts we have been given, and how we have been able to use them in the past, is part of our thankfulness to God. A strong sense of humility is appropriate, but failing to use our gift of understanding or wisdom when asked to contribute to decisions is an abrogation of responsibility.

6. **Listen to your heart.** Sometimes we are troubled about a decision and have no inner peace about it. When we do have a sense of inner peace, we are more likely to have reached the right decision. Paul told the Philippians, "The peace of God, which transcends all understanding, will guard your hearts and your minds in Christ Jesus" (Philippians 4:7). Gordon Smith wrote in *The Voice of Jesus* that discernment is learned over time as we come to recognize the movement of God in our hearts. Smith speaks of coming with open hearts before the truth so that we are fully engaged with the Spirit of the living God.[7]

---

7.   Gordon T. Smith, *The Voice of Jesus: Discernment, Prayer and the Witness of the Spirit* (Downers Grove, IL: InterVarsity, 2003), 64, 127.

7. **Engage with others.** Learning through engaging with others is about engaging both with our natural allies and with those with whom we differ in view or approach. Finding a mentor, coach, or spiritual director who has experience in difficult decisions as a Christian can provide a sounding board and sense of encouragement. Jesus sent the disciples out in pairs, recognizing their need for mutual encouragement and support. Sharpening our understanding also comes from engaging with those with whom we disagree, as Jesus did on frequent occasions.

8. **Pray continually.** If prayer is about being in the presence of God, finding time and energy to be focused in prayer is a priority when decisions are to be made. It may be an opportunity to reflect quietly on how Jesus might have approached a situation or on the relevance of one of the key Christian themes, such as forgiveness, compassion, hope, new life, or resurrection. Knowing what works best for you in a demanding period is important—so that through your preferred pattern of thoughts or words you become more reflective, with the emotional and busyness clutter diminished and the clarity of your thinking and prayerfulness enhanced. Seeking greater wisdom through prayer is a perfectly legitimate request and an essential part of Christian living.

9. **Spend time in a special place.** One of the gifts that Christian faith has brought to a wide range of people is the importance of special places. What are the places where your intellectual, emotional, and spiritual resources are best in harmony together? It might be when you are standing inside a majestic cathedral or a small chapel, walking through a field, sitting in a garden, or strolling beside pounding waves. When you need to make hard decisions, going to special

places can put you in a frame of mind in which you see the issues more clearly.

10. **Be open to being surprised.** The disciples were continually taken by surprise by the words and actions of Jesus, and they only gradually understood the full purpose of his ministry. As we prepare to make decisions, an openness to being surprised can bring new insights and perspectives. What may be needed is a combination of places and routines we know well, alongside an openness to new thinking. Allow yourself to be surprised by what you see and observe, and then view those surprises as if the risen Christ is alongside you. Be ready for your understanding of God's purposes to continue to grow as you are open to God who has created us; to Jesus, whose life and work continue to be relevant today; and to the Holy Spirit, who is never far from us.

There are important pitfalls to avoid in making hard decisions:

- Beware of those playing the "God card" as a means of avoiding the issue and trying to get their own way.
- Do not assume that bringing a Christian perspective makes it easier to make decisions; it can make it harder because you see a wider set of perspectives.
- Watch out for the notion that using your mental and emotional gifts when weighing a decision is somehow a poorer approach than direct ministry from the Holy Spirit. The Holy Spirit normally works through our mental faculties, not contrary to them.

Drawing from our human and Christian experiences is about allowing ourselves to be transformed so that hard decisions do not fill us with fear. Progress means stepping out and believing we can make hard decisions that are true to our values. We should never expect making hard decisions to be easy. If making hard decisions were easy, we would not be doing it well. A touch of uncertainty or vulnerability is vital to keeping our level of sensitivity high so that we never become complacent when hard decisions have to be made.

Being radical when making decisions may be about stepping out more boldly than we might at first have anticipated. It might mean having a picture of the risen Christ in our minds as we live through uncertainty.

APPLYING CHRISTIAN PRINCIPLES AT WORK

The Christian Association of Business Executives (CABE) is a fellowship of Christians who share common concerns, offer mutual support, and seek to promote the application of Christian principles in the working environment. In 2005 CABE, thanks to the leadership of chairman John McLean-Fox, put together a set of principles embracing corporate responsibility and personal values drawn from a Christian perspective. The document, reproduced in figure 7, set out thirty-one principles—the number chosen in order to reflect on one principle each day of the month.

The principles set out by CABE cover priority aims, corporate values, and personal qualities. They have provided an excellent basis for reflection and discussion by Christians in a broad range of organizations and countries. Appreciation for these principles have included the fact that (1) they reinforce the importance of Christians contributing at a corporate level within an organization; (2) they emphasize the importance of wider concerns such as community and environmental interests and stewardship; (3) they recognize the importance of an organization's responsibility to help maintain effective life balance for its employees; and (4) they demonstrate an effective balance between hard-edged values like commitment, courage, and justice and soft-edged values like joyfulness, care, and forgiveness.

Figure 7

PRINCIPLES FOR THOSE IN BUSINESS
CHRISTIAN ASSOCIATION OF BUSINESS EXECUTIVES

Priority Aims

1. **"Serve wholeheartedly**, as if you were serving the Lord, not men and women, because you know that the Lord will reward everyone for whatever good he does."—Ephesians 6:7–8

2. **Strive for Excellence**: As leaders we strive for excellence in all that we undertake, and aim to play a full part in contributing to the overall success of an organisation. We are serving God directly through carrying out such activities effectively, as well as the actual business in which we work; it may be a strictly commercial organisation, a public service or a not-for-profit charity.

3. **Create Wealth**: We affirm the principle of wealth creation as a process through which the resulting economic prosperity has the potential for benefiting humanity throughout the world. However, we shall challenge whether the particular form of wealth creation in which we engage is contributing to the Kingdom of God. Within a single business, we aim to fulfil our role in achieving acceptable financial and operating returns that will benefit appropriately all stakeholders in business.

4. **Achieve Targets**: We strive to assist in developing and setting targets for business goals which, when achieved, will lead to a successful and sustainable business. We aim to contribute personally to a successful financial outcome through target achievement by our own endeavours. We shall uphold the principle of wealth creation by taking all possible steps to achieve optimum business results, whether commercially or not-for-profit.

5. **Attain Vision**: Healthy organisations have a strong and shared vision for the future of their business. We seek to contribute to a strategic vision for whichever organisation we belong to and intend to help optimise the way forward for this business and its employees. We hope to be visionary in the expression and witness of our personal faith in Christ.

6. **Work Ethically**: Business ethics are essential in guiding employees and managers in their actions. Leading businesses care how results are obtained and will choose the course of highest integrity in guiding their affairs, avoiding such malpractices as price collusions. Honesty is not subject to criticism in any culture. Compliance with the law, and required business accounting regulation and practice, will be the duty of each employee.

Corporate Values

7. **Trust** lies at the heart of any successful and enduring personal or business relationship, so each organisation will do everything possible to establish and maintain the trust of all its stakeholders. We strive both as individuals and leaders to build trust within our teams, particularly as Managers and Directors, and aim to take specific steps to achieve this vital objective.

8. **Customer relationships** are of primary significance for any business. Success depends on the ability to satisfy ever-changing customer needs. We expect to be innovative and responsive while delivering high quality goods and services. We will respond to customers' complaints effectively and with seriousness and respect. We seek to safeguard in confidence all customer information, both corporate and personal.

9. **Employees** create the distinctive competence and capability of each organisation. We seek to develop imaginative, fair employee policies that will encourage colleagues to work effectively, and to find real meaning and purpose in their roles that will embrace body, mind and spirit. We aim to be open and honest with all staff members, and seek to reinforce clear and fair terms of employment and related remuneration. Through establishing supportive relationships we aim to show our concern and help motivate team members. We expect to provide equal opportunity in the workplace and encourage staff to develop new skills and progress their careers.

10. **Diversity**: We are committed to maintaining a workplace enriched by diversity, and characterised by open communication, trust and fair treatment for all employees, business partners or visitors irrespective of race/colour, gender, age, sexual orientation, class, creed or education.

11. **Providers of capital** play an essential part in the successful business. We seek to enhance the long term value of our business by running it responsibly and successfully, so that this participation will be rewarded fairly and appropriately. We shall contribute fully to the achievement of the financial success of the business so that this objective may be realised.

12. **Suppliers** depend on sales to the business for their commercial prosperity, and we expect to establish open and honest working relationships with all suppliers. Our aim is that each supplier should provide a high quality and reliable service for the goods and services procured, at an acceptable price. We seek to pay suppliers in accordance with agreed terms, and aim to procure goods and services from those who demonstrate good ethical practice.

13. **Community and environmental interests** are major concerns in society. We aim to encourage businesses to maintain appropriate environmental standards and to pay due attention to the specific interests of the local community. We strive to conduct business in accord with applicable environmental laws and regulations, while seeking to improve environmental performance. In addition, we expect to encourage business to develop and implement realistic, corporate, social responsibility programmes that will be demonstrably beneficial to the wider community.

14. **Stewardship**, making the best possible use of and conserving scarce resources, is a vital objective from both a corporate and an individual perspective. This presents an opportunity for creative solutions in given situations, and possibly the adoption of counter cultural approaches that will avoid waste and use resources more sparingly through some form of recycling.

15. **Corporate Reputation**: A well founded reputation for scrupulous dealings with customers, employees, investors and suppliers is a priceless asset. Such reputations depend on the effective leadership of Directors and Managers in relation to employees and the external bodies representing stakeholder interests. Businesses should take every opportunity to implement ethical practices and to introduce imaginative external initiatives. Such reputable practices, with a demonstrable commitment to quality, should form part of every Annual Report.

16. **Life balance** continues to be a struggle for everyone in today's world of work. The challenge is to achieve a balance between commitment to the organisation and to family, local church, community and life beyond work. Accepting that no perfect solution is possible, we strive to enable a fair allocation of commitment, time and energy between these varying demands. We aim to persuade senior colleagues to adopt family-friendly working practices, and we expect, as a leader, to apply this flexibility within our own area of responsibility.

Personal Qualities

17. **Personal Behaviour**: "As God's chosen ones, holy and beloved, clothe yourselves with compassion, kindness, humility, meekness and patience. Bear with one another and, if anyone has a complaint against another, forgive each other; just as the Lord has forgiven you, so you must also forgive. Above all, clothe yourselves with love which binds everything together in perfect harmony. And let the peace of Christ rule in your hearts, to which indeed you were called in the one body. And be thankful."—Colossians 3:12–17

18. **Commitment**: We aim to be faithful and committed in all the tasks and roles that we undertake, adopting an approach that is actively supported by prayer. We seek to balance this commitment in relation to the various calls upon our time, so that each aspect of our lives is allocated a fair span of energy and attention. It is our aim to demonstrate personal integrity in all such decisions we take, aiming to serve one another with humility, which admits that we have nothing that we have not received and acknowledges our insufficiency.

19. **Serving others** will be a hallmark of our lives, balanced by a choice of priorities that determine which individuals or group of people are appropriate for our personal attention at any given time. We always seek to be genuinely interested in the lives of the people we meet and discern their needs. This may lead us to make a sacrificial choice through opting for the least attractive alternative when faced with competing demands.

20. **Courage**: We seek to follow the strength of our convictions rather than accept automatically the views and decisions that are put to us. We are prepared to face opposition firmly based on these heartfelt and tested convictions, but strive to find bridges which provide solutions that are generally acceptable to others. This quality requires an underlying strength and preparedness to speak out for the truth. We draw on our faith to affirm a stand that may be unpopular, but which we believe to be the right course of action to be taken.

21. **Justice**: In each situation we meet we aim to exercise justice, and to discern the appropriate balancing of rights and claims in a given human context. We recognise fairness to be a concept that is good in itself, since it calls on us to put ourselves in the place of others and act accordingly: "Do to others as you would have them to do you." We seek to reach conclusions that are unselfish and tempered by moderation, involving self-control to deter us from exerting undue personal influence.

22. **Openness and honesty** in all dealings is a key aim, so that this will stimulate trust in every encounter. We strive to avoid deceitful actions and to display integrity in all the activities with which we are involved. We seek to build a personal reputation for trust and reliability, so that there may be a genuine responsiveness in situations with others that might otherwise be fraught. It is our aim to be known as someone who is entirely reliable and upon whom one can depend in times of difficulty.

23. **Resourcefulness**: We endeavour to respond positively to whatever events and occurrences that may befall us even if completely unexpected and critical in nature, such as an accident or explosion. We believe that our inner faith will give us a resilience to address such situations pragmatically, and enable us to assess priorities for assisting those adversely affected. We rely on our faith to provide us with a positive outlook even in the darkest of circumstances, seeing that our life view is set in the context of eternity rather than the current moment.

24. **Creativity**: Inherent in the majority of human beings is the capability to think beyond the confines of everyday existence; we support a view that takes advantage of this God-given creativity. We believe that such creativity draws upon the latent talents and skills that lie below the surface and is essentially a force for good. We recognise that progress is normally achieved through the introduction of new concepts, and that this can bring with it the need for change, which can be painful.

25. **Joyfulness**, which we hope will be demonstrated through the grace and beauty of divine joy in our lives. We delight in fun and laughter, rejoicing in the world, its beauty and its living creatures. We aim to mix freely with all people, ready to bind up the broken-hearted, and to bring joy into the lives of others. We strive to carry within us an upper peace and happiness which others may perceive, even if they do not know its source.

26. **Care**: We aim to show a sympathetic response to all we meet during the course of our professional and business lives. Inspired as disciples by love, we seek to practice an ongoing caring relationship with work colleagues, family and friends. Where it may be necessary to take tough decisions in our work, the implications for those affected will never be far from our thoughts. Wherever possible we seek to ameliorate adverse effects of decisions and endeavour to give gladly of ourselves, remembering that genuine love frequently involves sacrifice.

27. **Forgiveness**: We aim to practice a forgiving approach when experiencing painful opposition or personal attacks. It will be our intention to adopt a conciliatory approach that, despite implicit rights or wrongs, will enable the particular event to be set aside and forgotten, so that the parties involved may move on. If this may mean that difficult personal exchanges will be necessary, we see it as beneficial to come to terms with the reality of each situation for those issues to be resolved.

28. **Prayerfulness**: We seek through prayer to discern the divine will for our lives; we recognise that we cannot fulfil these aims unless our lives are supported by prayer. We use prayer as the means of communicating with God and seek to pray regularly, whether daily in specific times of prayer or from time to time in our working lives. Our purpose will be both to listen to God and to offer given situations for His blessing. We aim to give ourselves the necessary time to make such prayers possible, and regard attention to prayer as a priority for our personal, spiritual development.

---

29. **Interpersonal Behaviour:** "Love must be sincere. Hate what is evil; cling to what is good. Be devoted to one another in brotherly love. Honour one another above yourselves. Never be lacking in zeal, but keep your spiritual fervour, serving the Lord. Be joyful in hope, patient in affliction, faithful in prayer. Share with God's people who are in need. Practice hospitality."—Romans 12:9–13

---

30. **Maintaining Personal Integrity:** We are committed, in the face of so many temptations, distractions and personal difficulties that beset us, to remain true to ourselves and to faith in our God. We are reminded that nothing whatsoever can separate us from the love of Christ, and we are determined to live our lives according to our perception of God's will for us personally.

---

31. **Contributing Financially:** We all expect to give generously when discharging our community responsibilities, based on the widely recognised principle of tithing. For those of us who are highly paid because of market circumstances, we strive to give a disproportionately higher level of our assets and income to community or charitable ventures that we feel committed to or are inspired by.

Used by permission.

The application of these principles will vary, to an extent, depending on the context and the culture. But as you reflect on the set of principles in figure 7 . . .

- Do any of the principles surprise you? If so, how do you want to respond to that surprise?
- In which of the principles are you strong, and in which do you feel you have made less progress?
- Which two or three principles would you like to work on more? What will your next steps be?
- How will you hold yourself accountable to take some of these principles to the next stage?

Reflecting on Christian principles and how they apply at work can be a very useful prompt in the way we use our time and energy. Looking at which two or three principles you want to work on can provide an opportunity for reflection and eventually a new balance point. Sometimes there might be an opportunity to be more radical. For example:

- Is there a principle that you want to speak out about?
- Is there a specific cause—for example, relief or

environmental issues—into which you would like to put a good deal of effort and energy?

- Is there a need in your local community in which you may be able to provide effective input, thereby transforming an otherwise depressing situation for some individuals?

Doing something radical may be consistent with your current full-time job. Or it could mean shifting to part-time, taking a leave of absence for a period of time, or resigning altogether. Taking radical action may not necessarily lead to the conclusion you first assumed; indeed, it might mean continuing where you are. But having thought through the options, you may well become more focused and invigorated to provide leadership within your current sphere.

BEING AN EFFECTIVE PART OF A TEAM

The Bible commands us to "love your neighbor as yourself," but Christians often find it surprisingly difficult to work well together. I was recently involved in putting together a series of talks on this subject that had the following elements:

- Understanding each other—based on Jesus' relationship with Mary, Martha, and Lazarus (John 11:17–44)
- Trusting each other—based on Jesus and Peter (John 13:1–17)
- Learning together—based on the disciples as they followed Jesus (Matthew 10:1–20)
- Encouraging each other—based on Paul and Barnabas (Acts 14:1–20)
- Turning our differences to our advantage—based on Peter and Paul (Acts 15:1–31)
- Delivering outcomes together—based on the work of Paul and Silas (Acts 16:16–40)

A continued focus on understanding each other is an essential part of keeping a team working well. The interaction of Jesus with Mary, Martha, and Lazarus is about the interactions of four very different people. When Lazarus died, Jesus visited the family. Martha rushed out to meet Jesus and talk to him, but Mary stayed in the house and only came out to see Jesus when Martha pressed her to do so. Then she came weeping, which deeply moved Jesus.

When Jesus visited the family on a later occasion (John 12:1–3), we see again the differences in the siblings. Lazarus listened to Jesus, though no words of his were recorded. Maybe he was a listener and reflector. Martha, as she had done on other occasions (see Luke 10:38–40), prepared a dinner in Jesus' honor. Mary took expensive perfume and poured it on Jesus' feet and wiped his feet with her hair. Martha's cooking would have filled the house with the delectable smells of good food. Mary's generosity filled the house with the fragrance of perfume.

The sisters were making different yet complementary contributions. Martha was a go-getter: immediately rushing out to see Jesus, talking to him, cooking a large meal. Mary was quieter and more emotional, having a sensitivity to Jesus' needs and playing her part through the generosity of the giving of her perfume in preparation for Jesus' death and resurrection. The siblings did not usually complain about each other; they appeared to accept each other's differences.

John Winthrop was the first governor of the Massachusetts Bay Colony. In a sermon to his fellow Puritan colonists just before they stepped foot on land in 1630, he said, "We must delight in each other, make others' conditions our own, rejoice together, mourn together, labour and suffer together, always having before our eyes our community as members of the same body." Today's work context may seem very different, but the words of John Winthrop can still ring true for us.

When Sir Edmund Hillary and Tenzing Norgay became the first mountain climbers in history to scale Mount Everest, they had to have complete trust in each other and in the backup team. They had to trust that there was adequate food, oxygen, and supplies. Mutual support needed to be part of the way the whole expedition worked together.

The interactions of Jesus and Peter included strong expressions of commitment from Peter, together with moments of uncertainty and denial. The trust between Jesus and Peter, which took time to develop and had its ups and downs, was built on shared experiences. Their relationship involved openness and a willingness on Peter's part to admit mistakes. Above all, their relationship was based on a shared love and sense of purpose.

Likewise, in the teams in which I have been a part:

- Trust takes time to develop and needs to be built on shared experiences.
- Trust will have its ups and downs, as none of us are perfect; we will feel let down, and we will let other people down, but that is not the end of the story.
- Trust requires that we keep talking, listening, and responding, as well as demonstrating that we have been listening.
- Trust is based on people wanting to work together and working through hard issues.
- Trust involves openness and saying what we think. Far better the courteous expression of unhappiness rather than the insidious muttering of discontent.
- Trust is based on a shared love and sense of purpose, so that the gospel message of love, sacrifice, and new birth is evidenced in what we do as individuals and as a Christian community.
- And, finally, trust entails admitting that we make mistakes.

Patrick Lencioni has written a leadership fable called *The Five Dysfunctions of a Team*. He summarizes the five dysfunctions in the following way:

1. The first dysfunction is an *absence of trust* among team

members. This stems from their unwillingness to be vulnerable with the group. Team members who are not genuinely open with one another about their mistakes and weaknesses make it impossible to build a foundation for trust.

2. This failure to build trust is damaging because it sets the tone for the second dysfunction: *fear of conflict*. Teams that lack trust are incapable of engaging in unfiltered and passionate debate of ideas. Instead, they resort to veiled discussions and guarded comments.

3. A lack of healthy conflict is a problem because it ensures the third dysfunction of a team: *lack of commitment*. Without having aired their opinions in the course of passionate and open debate, team members rarely, if ever, buy in and commit to decisions, though they may feign agreement during meetings.

4. Because of this lack of real commitment and buy-in, team members develop an *avoidance of accountability*, the fourth dysfunction. Even the most focused and driven people can then hesitate to challenge their peers on actions and behaviors that seem counterproductive to the good of the team.

5. Failure to hold one another accountable creates an environment where the fifth dysfunction can thrive. *Inattention to results* occurs when team members put their individual needs (such as ego, career, development, or recognition), or even the needs of their divisions, above the collective goals of the team.[8]

And so, like a chain with just one link broken, teamwork deteriorates if even a single dysfunction is allowed to flourish.

---

8.   Patrick Lencioni, *The Five Dysfunctions of a Team: A Leadership Fable* (San Francisco: Jossey-Bass, 2002).

Another way to apply this model is to take the opposite approach—a positive one—and imagine how members of truly cohesive teams behave:

1. They trust one another.
2. They engage in unfiltered conflict around ideas.
3. They commit to decisions and plans of action.
4. They hold one another accountable for delivering against those plans.
5. They focus on the achievement of collective results.

As you reflect on the team of which you are part:

- How do you score this team (0 = poor to 5 = strong) on trust, positive use of conflict, commitment, accountability, and attention to results?
- What influence can you bring to improve these areas?
- What would help improve the dynamics of the team?
- What might be key milestones along the way, and how can you build allies to help ensure progress?

When we play our part as a team member, we won't always get it right. We can sometimes be the cause of dysfunction and disharmony by being insensitive to other people. Ensuring we have effective feedback about the contribution we make is vital to reinforcing how we can best make a successful contribution. Key questions to ask yourself might be:

- How good are you at understanding where other people are coming from in their respective contributions?
- What role do you play in different teams, and how can you enhance your contribution as a team member through your approach and actions?

Being radical when leading a team might involve being bold in how team members are selected and how they are encouraged to develop their contributions outside of their comfort zones. It might mean being open to testing out different approaches to building trust in a team and being willing to share your own vulnerabilities.

WHAT IS YOUR PROFILE AS A CHRISTIAN AT WORK?

I came across a variety of views on this theme. All the people I spoke to were clear that when asked at work if they are a Christian they would be explicit in their response, but there were a variety of views about how overt they would be in volunteering their Christian faith.

One military leader was clear: "I am explicit about my faith. People need to understand the driving force in my life." Others were more inclined to rely on their general demeanor and approach and to be ready to respond to questions, but not to be directly explicit about their faith.

Another military leader talked about not wearing his faith on his sleeve but being ready to say, "I do this because I am a Christian." His advice is not to be afraid about talking about your faith and offering to pray for someone. For him there is joy in being open and honest about his faith. He stressed the importance of respecting other people's views when you are in a leadership position: when you relate to people junior to you, it is appropriate to be open about your faith but not to create expectations on others because of your faith.

Another leader stressed the importance of being on guard against any sense of being superior or separating yourself. This means relying much more on your deeds than your words and only using words "if you must."

My own experience as a director general in government was that I was always willing to be open about my faith and my involvement as an Anglican reader (that is, a licensed lay minister). I was happy to talk about what I had been doing at church over the weekend. There were opportunities to talk reflectively with people at key moments in their lives, but I never felt it was right to force my faith on them. A fellow board member who went on to a very senior position was a committed member of the Jewish faith; we found that we had a lot in common and used to have good conversations about the relevance of a faith perspective in a variety of different situations.

I once worked in the same organization as a technical specialist who was a committed Christian and who would, at any opportunity, stop working to talk about his faith. The results were that his work didn't get done and that his reputation was severely tarnished. He saw his work as a wonderful opportunity to evangelize others. Many people viewed him as abusing the system and creating more work for others because he failed to do his job properly. From my perspective this individual did more harm than good, as his approach to Christianity became regarded as opportunistic and irresponsible. There is an important dividing line between this type of behavior and being responsive to your colleagues in the workplace by taking the opportunities that present themselves to support and encourage them and help them in their faith journey. Those who get this balance right will be fully committed to their work but find opportunities at lunchtime or at other times of the day to encourage or "minister" to their colleagues.

I remember working with a senior leader whom I had always respected. We had a very difficult piece of negotiating to do, and I was impressed by his thoughtfulness and willingness to reach a sensible outcome. I had expected him to be very difficult to negotiate with and was pleasantly surprised by the way he brought firmness and a desire to find the best way forward. A number of years later I learned that he is a committed Christian; everything then fell into place as to why he had taken the responsible approach he did in those difficult negotiations. He didn't wear his faith on his sleeve, but it clearly influenced the way he worked with others.

For some the focus of their ministry is within the local church or Christian community. Time is spent in the workplace solely in order to provide an income stream to enable them to do "Christian work." Such a separation between work and Christian commitment outside work can mean missing out on opportunities to influence others in the workplace. By our approach and demeanor we can have a profound influence in the workplace on the way decisions are made and the level of goodwill and mutual encouragement that exists within the organization. Through their contribution to decision making, many Christians have brought stability and equilibrium to different types of organizations. This contribution is not to be underestimated.

There is a greater openness in many organizations to those who bring a faith perspective. There is an acceptance of the practices and disciplines held by Muslim, Hindu, Sikh, and Jewish staff members. That openness and respect apply just as much to those who come with a Christian perspective. There can be a common cause in the workplace between those of different faith perspectives when it comes to encouraging and reinforcing particular values or behaviors. The acceptance of the fact that discrimination on grounds of religion is wrong in legal and moral terms can provide a stronger foundation for the Christian in the workplace than a couple of decades ago.

Key questions to ask might be:
- How high or low is your profile as a Christian at work?
- Do you take advantage of opportunities to influence others in terms of appropriate values and behaviors in the workplace?
- In what circumstances do you share about your Christian faith in the workplace?
- What is the right balance for you in the future in terms of how explicit you are about your faith and when you would choose to talk about it?

WORKING EFFECTIVELY WITH THOSE OF OTHER FAITHS
As an executive coach, I work with Christian leaders in a variety of different contexts, and I also thoroughly enjoy working with Sikh,

Muslim, and Hindu leaders. Leaders who share the importance of a faith perspective, albeit a different faith, often have far more in common than do those with no faith. When people of different faiths are on the same team, finding shared values can provide an important foundation for how team members are going to work together.

One military leader commented, "I have found you are not at odds from the word *go*. There is a sense of shared spirituality and a bond there. It is important not to be alarmed by the faith of others. As a commanding officer in Bosnia, I found I got on well with the imams I met. There was one imam I used to have long conversations with. He loved discussions about matters of faith. We are maybe too backward in sharing our views with people of other faiths."

With increased globalization, people of different faiths will often be on the same team. This reinforces the importance of building an understanding of what people believe—and why—and of building a shared view about how best to work together. This is not about pretending differences do not exist. It is about defining as clearly as possible the common ground that enables people to work together effectively, while recognizing there will be differences of belief and practice that have to be tolerated.

A number of global organizations have been willing to give high profile to the importance of building clarity about religious understanding. For example, Goldman Sachs in London has held "diversity days" when religion has been the topic. On one such occasion, George Carey, the former archbishop of Canterbury, and a rabbi were asked to address three questions: (1) What does your faith say? (2) What does your faith say about work? (3) What does your faith say about the wider society? These events have attracted many people, demonstrating a keen interest in building a greater understanding of this subject.

When I have observed people of different faiths working together effectively, it has typically been because there have been mutual respect;

an openness to other people's views; a willingness to engage others and understand why they hold their views; and a recognition of the practical reality that the team has to work together effectively, using the skills and perspectives of all the team members, whether or not they come from a faith perspective.

Questions to ask yourself might be:
- How willing are you to understand the perspective of those who come from a different faith background?
- On what level are you willing to engage with those who are committed members of another faith?
- Do you intentionally seek out people who come from different faiths so that you can better understand their convictions?
- How eagerly would you welcome the prospect of working with someone from a different faith? If the opportunity arises, how willing would you be to share your own faith as you learn about his or her faith perspective?

BEING SALT AND LIGHT AT WORK

In the Sermon on the Mount in Matthew's Gospel, immediately after the Beatitudes Jesus refers to his followers as the salt of the earth and the light of the world:

> You are the salt of the earth. But if the salt loses its saltiness, how can it be made salty again? It is no longer good for anything, except to be thrown out and trampled underfoot.
>
> You are the light of the world. A city on a hill cannot be hidden. Neither do people light a lamp and put it under a bowl. Instead they put it on its stand, and it gives light to everyone in the house. In the same way, let your light shine before others, that they may see your good deeds and glorify your Father in heaven.—Matthew 5:13–16

The metaphors of salt and light provide powerful descriptions of the radical contribution that a Christian is called to bring. Sometimes that contribution is like salt, which, though all-pervasive, may be hidden. On other occasions it is like light, which is very overt.

Dick France, in his commentary on Matthew, speaks of salt serving mainly to give flavor and to prevent corruption. He suggests that disciples of Jesus, if they are true to their calling, make the earth a purer and more palatable place. But they can do so only as long as they preserve their distinctive character; unsalty salt no longer has value. The rabbis commonly used salt as an image for wisdom, which may explain why the Greek word represented by "lost its taste" actually means "become foolish."[9]

France likewise refers to light affecting its environment by being distinctive. He suggests that disciples who are visibly different from others will have an effect on them. The aim of Christians, however, is not to parade their own virtue but to direct attention to the God who inspired them.[10]

In his commentary entitled *Matthew for Everyone*, Tom Wright refers to this passage as a kind of gateway to all that follows. He wrote, "God had called Israel to be the salt of the earth; but Israel was behaving like everyone else, with its power politics, its factional squabbles, its military revolutions. How could God keep the world from going bad—the main function of salt in the ancient world—if Israel, his chosen 'salt,' had lost its distinctive taste?"[11]

Wright continues:

> In the same way, God called Israel to be the light of the world (e.g., Isaiah 42:6 and 49:6). Israel was the people through

---

9.   R. T. France, *Matthew* (Leicester, UK: Inter-Varsity, 1985), 112.

10.   Ibid., 112–13.

11.   Tom Wright, *Matthew for Everyone: Part 1: Chapters 1–15* (London: SPCK Publishing, 2002), 40.

whom God intended to shine his bright light into the world's dark corners, not simply to show up evil but to enable people who were blundering around in the dark to find their way. But what if the people called to be the light-bearers had become part of the darkness? That was Jesus' warning—and also his challenge. Jerusalem, the city on the hill, was supposed to be a beacon of hope to the world. His followers were to be like that: their deep, heartfelt keeping of God's laws would be a sign to the nations around that the one God, the Creator, the God of Israel, was God indeed, and that they should worship him.[12]

This exhortation to be salt and light was right at the center of living the Beatitudes. As Tom Wright observes, it was the "gateway" to fulfilled Christian living and impact.

Christians in the workplace are being salt, giving flavor, preserving what is good, and preventing corruption. Christians are called to bring light, which pertains to vision, openness, and a sense of direction.

Eddie Donaldson, who has held senior roles in an international audit and advisory organization, identifies the critical importance of Christians being salt and light—being used by God in different ways at different times. Sometimes Eddie was called upon to be salt: that is, being a peacemaker and bringing harmony within a senior team. Sometimes it was right to be light: for example, when he started a prayer breakfast in the organization when he was quite junior, which meant putting his head above the parapet.[13]

During an interview Eddie commented, "I see the themes of salt and light as absolutely critical. These themes illustrate how God works through us. If we withdraw, we constrain the ability of God at work.

---

12. Ibid.
13. "Putting your head above the parapet" is an expression meaning to be brave enough to take an action that might put you in danger or upset other people.

Sometimes we are there as salt, where the influence can be great but sometimes unseen. On the other occasions we are called to be light, when we need to be bolder about what should happen."

Can I invite you to reflect on what being salt and light in your workplace might mean? Do you bring a sort of saltiness, or has the saltiness dispersed? Is the light that you bring hidden under a bowl? Jesus' exhortation is that we let our light shine before others so that they see the good we are able to do in a way that brings glory to God.

Specific questions to reflect upon might be:
- To what extent have you been salt in your workplace?
- In what ways, over the next few months, can you be like salt: bringing flavor, preserving what is good, and preventing corruption or disruption?
- To what extent are you a source of light within your organization?
- Is there more light that you can bring?

CONCLUSION

In this second section we have looked at what it means for the Christian leader to be radical. We have focused on the importance of role models, living with economic and global change, identifying critical leadership attributes in the future, building vision and values in organizations, making hard decisions well, applying Christian principles at work, being an effective part of a team, being clear about your profile as a Christian in the workplace, working effectively with those of other faiths, and seeing the contribution of the Christian in the workplace as bringing salt and light.

Here are some final reflections:
- Enjoy observing role models, and be clear what you are going to embed from that experience.
- View economic and global change as an opportunity rather than a threat.

- Be open-minded about discovering and implementing important leadership attributes in the future.
- Be willing to share your Christian convictions when your organization is reflecting on its vision and values.
- Accept that making hard decisions well is part of your Christian responsibility.
- Carefully think through how you are going to apply your Christian principles at work.
- Be ready to bring a dynamic contribution as a member of a team.
- Allow your imagination to reflect on what being salt and light in the workplace means. Enable the Holy Spirit to speak through you. Then be willing to be salt and light, recognizing that this will be accepted and welcomed by some but rejected or ignored by others.
- Above all, be willing to be radical, just as Jesus was radical.

REFLECTIVE

We have looked at being rooted and radical. We now turn to being reflective. It is in being reflective that we strike the right balance between being rooted and radical. Being reflective includes starting with Christian character, listening and dialoguing effectively, asking the right questions, getting the balance right, and handling risks well. Being reflective involves valuing mentoring, ensuring effective feedback, knowing attributes to avoid, and living with our imperfections. It enables us to take stock of our vocation and the interrelationship between our work and faith. It is in living the Beatitudes that we bring depth and richness to our lives as Christians in a global and secular world.

WHY IS IT IMPORTANT TO BE REFLECTIVE?

There is a danger that we can be so rooted that we are not radical enough or so radical that we are not rooted. Being reflective is the quality that holds us in the right balance between being rooted and radical. As we reflect, we see the context more clearly and understand the role we can play more effectively. Part of being reflective is letting our unconscious do the thinking—enabling God's Spirit within us to commune with our own inner being so that we become clearer in our own minds as to the correct next step or the appropriate way of thinking and responding.

Being reflective is not an excuse for inaction. Rather it is allowing ourselves to have the space and time to let our spiritual, emotional, and physical awareness sit alongside each other so that we become more rooted and radical in a way that is intellectually and spiritually robust. Being reflective is a means of reaching a clarity of mind about next steps that is neither simplistic nor illusory.

STARTING WITH CHRISTIAN CHARACTER

The ability to reflect effectively starts when we are clear about our character and the influence of our Christian faith upon that character. In its leadership course entitled "Growing Leaders," CPAS (Church Pastoral Aid Society) describes the following as the marks of Christlike character:

- Jesus, leader of love, looks for leaders of love (1 John 4:8–12; 1 Corinthians 16:14).
- Jesus, leader of integrity, looks for leaders of integrity (Hebrews 4:14–16; Matthew 19:16–26).
- Jesus, a leader who served, looks for leaders with a servant heart (Luke 22:7–38).
- Jesus, a leader of compassion, looks for leaders of compassion (John 11:35; Luke 7:11–17; Luke 18:35–43).
- Jesus, a leader of truth, looks for leaders of truth (Matthew 5:37).
- Jesus, a leader of faith, looks for leaders of faith (Mark 14:36; 1 Corinthians 4:2).
- Jesus, a leader of forgiveness, looks for leaders of forgiveness (Matthew 6:14–15).
- Jesus, a leader of humility, looks for humble leaders (Philippians 2:5–11; John 13:1–7).

The "Growing Leaders" material lists the characteristics of godly leadership in the following figure:

Figure 8

Characteristics of Godly Leadership		
A servant's heart	Honesty	Loyalty
Perseverance	Trustworthiness	Courage
Humility	Sensitivity	Teachability
Values-driven	Optimism	Even-tempered
Joy	Gentleness	Consistency
Spiritual depth	Forgiveness	Compassion
Energy	Faithfulness	Self-control
Love	Wisdom	Discernment
Encouraging	Passion	Fairness
Patience	Kindness	Mercy
Reliability	Fun	Integrity
CPAS "Growing Leaders" Program (used by permission)		

The course also explores the following passage from 2 Peter, which refers to qualities of Christian leadership, namely goodness, knowledge, self-control, perseverance, godliness, mutual affection, and love.

Simon Peter, a servant and apostle of Jesus Christ,

To those who through the righteousness of our God and Savior Jesus Christ have received a faith as precious as ours:

Grace and peace be yours in abundance through the knowledge of God and of Jesus our Lord.

His divine power has given us everything we need for a godly life through our knowledge of him who called us by his own glory and goodness. Through these he has given us his very great and precious promises, so that through them you may participate in the divine nature, having escaped the corruption in the world caused by evil desires.

For this very reason, make every effort to add to your faith goodness; and to goodness, knowledge; and to knowledge, self-control; and to self-control, perseverance; and to perseverance, godliness; and to godliness, mutual affection; and to mutual affection, love. For if you possess these qualities in increasing measure, they will keep you from being ineffective and unproductive in your knowledge of our Lord Jesus Christ. But if any of you do not have them, you are nearsighted and blind, and you have forgotten that you have been cleansed from your past sins.

Therefore, my brothers and sisters, make every effort to confirm your calling and election. For if you do these things, you will never stumble, and you will receive a rich welcome into the eternal kingdom of our Lord and Savior Jesus Christ.—2 Peter 1:1–11

Questions for reflection:
- Which of the characteristics of Christian leadership in 2 Peter 1 resonate most with you?
- Which elements together combine to produce a robust sense of Christian character and discipleship?
- Which three of the "characteristics of godly leadership" listed in the CPAS course are strengths upon which you would like to build further?
- Which three are areas where you are less strong and that you would like to develop?

The theme of reflection in this chapter encourages us to ask these types of questions in a measured and purposeful way. God has given us considerable strengths to recognize and develop. If we deny our strengths, we are denying the gifts that God has given us. But reflection also gives us the opportunity to be honest about the areas where we are less strong and perhaps need to grow our competencies and sensitivities further.

LISTENING AND ENGAGING EFFECTIVELY

Francis de Sales, who was a Roman Catholic bishop in the early seventeenth century, wrote, "Half an hour's listening is essential except when you are very busy. Then a full hour is needed." Most of us are familiar with the illustration that we are given two ears and only one tongue so that we might listen twice as much as we speak. Listening is the starting point for reflection.

Jesus' life was busy not only with teaching but also with listening, as we see in two illustrations from opposite ends of his life. On an occasion when he was twelve years old, Jesus was fully engaged with the teachers in the temple courts: he was listening to understand (see Luke 2:41–52). The teachers were fully engrossed, and as a consequence, the time passed quickly. All those present were enlivened by the conversation, amazed at Jesus' understanding and his answers. In listening to the teachers and questioning them, Jesus was growing in wisdom and stature. The starting point was listening, but there was full dialogue because of his understanding and answers.

After his resurrection, Jesus walked with two disciples on the road to Emmaus (see Luke 24:13–35). Jesus listened as they talked. He asked them open-ended questions about what they were discussing and then began a dialogue with them. He understood the source of their worries and concerns and shared reflections with them from his knowledge of the Old Testament Scriptures.

In these two situations Jesus was valuing people, asking questions, and listening to learn and to discern. He was fully engaged, brought objectivity, and "walked" alongside those with whom he was in dialogue.

Much has been written about the art of listening. Dietrich Bonhoeffer, a German pastor executed by the Nazi regime, wrote thoughtfully about listening. In his book *Life Together*, he wrote:

The first service that one owes to others in the fellowship consists of listening to them. Many people are looking for an ally that will listen. They do not find it among Christians, because these Christians are talking where they should be listening. But he who can no longer listen to his brothers will soon no longer be listening to God either; he will be doing nothing but prattle in the presence of God too. Anyone who cannot listen long and patiently will presently be talking beside the point and be never really speaking to others. There is a kind of listening with half an ear that presumes already to know what the other person has to say. It is an impatient, inattentive listening, that despises the brother and is only waiting for a chance to speak and thus get rid of the other person.[1]

Bonhoeffer's focus is that listening can be a greater service than speaking: "We should listen with the ears of God that we may speak the Word of God."[2]

In his foreword to Ann Long's influential book, *Listening*, Gerard Hughes notes that listening is an art that we can only acquire by practice. Long says that good listeners develop and grow by learning to reflect on the questions and difficulties that inevitably arise in the listening relationship. She describes the ministry of listening using the images of gift, hospitality, and healing.[3]

Long describes listening as being about hospitality: the offering to someone of space in which to feel welcomed, met, and safe; free to be themselves; free to be listened to and heard. Then she sets out six dimensions that make up a good listener's offering and skill:

---

1.   Dietrich Bonhoeffer, *Life Together* (New York: Harper and Row, 1954), 98.
2.   Ibid., 99.
3.   Ann Long, *Listening* (London: Darton, Longman and Todd, 1990).

- **Respect**: giving value to the other person, affirming him or her as unique.
- **Genuineness**: being real and open rather than playing a role and not play-acting at listening.
- **Empathy**: which is not "to feel like" but "to feel with." It is about seeing the world through the other person's eyes, being accurately aware of his or her feelings and attempting to put them into words.
- **Concreteness**: helping a person to be specific rather than vague.
- **Confrontation**: this is not about trying to make someone look bad, but it is about firmly and carefully enabling a person to become aware of the discrepancies in his or her thinking.
- **Immediacy**: which involves being fully aware of how you are being experienced as a listener. [4]

Henri Nouwen called listening the highest form of hospitality—hospitality of a sort that does not set out to change people but rather to offer them space where change can happen. The offering of personal space through listening enables healing to take place.

Jonathan Sacks wrote an article about listening in the *London Times*. He stated:

> What an underrated art listening is. Sometimes it is the greatest gift we can give to a troubled soul. It is an act of focused attention. It means being genuinely open to another person, prepared to enter their world, their perspective, their pain. It does not mean we have a solution to their problem. There are some problems that cannot be solved. They can only be lived through, so that time itself heals the rupture or loss. When we

---

4. Ibid.

listen we share the burden so its weight can be borne. There are times when friendship calls simply for a human presence, a listening ear and an understanding heart so that soul can unburden to soul.[5]

Effective listening is not about complete silence. In her excellent book, *The Art of Persuasion*, Juliet Erickson recommends the following as good practices of listening:

- **Validate.** Validating what someone has said makes the person feel good, while affirming that you have heard and understood what he or she is saying. We often withhold compliments because of embarrassment, stinginess, or thoughtlessness; but "What a good suggestion!" can be a very affirming comment during a conversation.

- **Pause.** Allow the other person time to think, to give a more considered answer. Pausing after his or her response can also encourage further dialogue.

- **Ask one question at a time.** Take a deep breath, slow down, and ask one question at a time if a deluge of questions floods into your mind.

- **Summarize.** Summaries are relevant not only at the end of a conversation but also at key points within a conversation. They can help mark the "completion" of parts of a conversation and allow for a smoother transition. They can also provide reassurance that as a listener you have heard and understood what has been said.[6]

Questions to consider might be:

- How good of a listener are you?
- What steps can you take to develop your listening skills?

---

5.   Jonathan Sacks, "Listening Is the Greatest Gift We Can Give to a Troubled Soul," *London Times*, December 14, 2002.
6.   Juliet Erickson, *The Art of Persuasion: How to Influence People and Get What You Want* (London: Hodder and Stoughton, 2004).

- What would be the benefits of becoming a more effective listener?

In my book *Conversation Matters: How to Engage Effectively with One Another*, I look at seven different types of conversations: listening, encouraging, challenging, short, painful, unresponsive, and joyful. Each one has its own dynamics and brings different emotions. Jesus engaged in all these different types of conversations, and I draw the following practical principles and pitfalls from his experiences.

I draw three elements from the way Jesus conducted conversations: engagement, discernment, and stretching. Engagement, which is based on building trust, includes confidentiality, openness, humor, communion, and a sense of traveling together and sharing space. Discernment is about clarity, asking good questions, curiosity, experimentation, and the willingness to take risks. Quality conversations stretch the thinking of those with whom you are in dialogue. Stretching conversations transcend boundaries and are dynamic; they bring challenge, freshness, and a compelling modesty.

Pitfalls to guard against include:
- Realize that words do not make all the difference; they are just part of the information your hearer is taking in.
- Watch out for inconsistency.
- Beware of initial impressions.
- Allow for changing phases in conversations.
- Be alert to differing expectations due to cultural differences.
- Beware of one-sided conversations.
- Recognize that successful conversations can be messy.

Conversations are a very important tool for a Christian in the secular world.
- Through conversations we define who we are and what matters to us.
- Through conversations we connect with others.

- Conversations offer us a chance to share and clarify our purpose.
- Conversations provide a context for fun, curiosity, and adventure.
- Conversations are enriched by variety: thoughtfulness, laughter, challenge, and encouragement are all important.
- Quietness in conversation provides a space for calmness within our key relationships.
- Through conversations we are responding to the reality that Christ's life was full of conversations.
- Conversations are crucial to how we relate to each other and to God.
- All conversations are an outworking of our willingness to listen.

Conversation is part of the way Jesus lived. He had an encouraging conversation with the Samaritan woman at the well, a challenging conversation with Nicodemus, a short initial conversation with Zacchaeus, a painful conversation with the rich young ruler, an unresponsive conversation with Judas when Judas came to betray him, and a joyful conversation with Mary after his resurrection. Jesus' life was full of varied conversations. Hence the encouragement to us to engage in conversations of different types with a variety of people. As we dialogue with others, we learn more about ourselves as well as those people. Conversation can be a great aid to reflection as we crystallize what is important to us.

Key questions to ask about your conversations might be:
- What type of Jesus' conversations resonate most with you?
- What sort of conversations do you particularly enjoy?
- When do you find conversation difficult, and how might you overcome this?
- With whom can you spend more time in conversation in a productive way?

- What value do you place on reflective conversation with the people who are precious to you?

THE HEART OF LEADERSHIP IS
ASKING THE RIGHT QUESTIONS

Essential to good listening and good conversation is the use of questions that elicit a thoughtful, open response. When a good question is asked, a genuine and worthwhile exchange takes place between two people. When you ask a good question, both you and the other person know you are listening.

Juliet Erickson suggests that asking questions is like a dance: If you do it wrong, you will tread on your partner's toes or otherwise embarrass that person. If you do it right, you will move together gracefully, and it will be a pleasure. Though you are doing the leading, your partner is hardly aware of the fact and is happy to follow.[7]

We live in a world full of information. We are drowned by facts, figures, pictures, and opinions. How does a leader make sense of this myriad of information? Do we just soak it up like a sponge and wait for it to be squeezed out of us? The ability to ask the right question in the right way at the right time can bring clarity to an otherwise confused world. The ability to ask the right question can bring a new focus leading to enlightenment about next steps.

In his book *Jesus Asked: What He Wanted to Know*, Conrad Gempf explores the way Jesus used questions.[8] The first recorded event in Jesus' life after his birth occurred at the temple when he sat with the Jewish teachers, listening to them and asking questions (Luke 2:41–49). In

7. Ibid.
8. Conrad Gempf, *Jesus Asked: What He Wanted to Know* (Grand Rapids: Zondervan, 2003).

the Gospels, we repeatedly find Jesus having conversations, and these frequently include Jesus asking questions.

Jesus employed a wide range of approaches. He would assert truth, tell parables, and paint word pictures. But fundamental to his approach was the use of questions of many different types. He didn't ask questions in order to acquire knowledge, but to initiate a conversation, to give people an occasion for a reply. Jesus used four types of approaches: the innocent question, the absurd question, the question in response to a question, and the challenging question.

The Innocent Question

Not all of Jesus' questions were full of symbolism. Some were part of daily life. Before healing a boy, Jesus asked his father, "How long has he been like this?" Before the feeding of the five thousand, Jesus asked his disciples, "How many loaves do you have?" As he walked with two disciples on the road to Emmaus after his resurrection, Jesus asked, "What are you discussing together as you walk along?" Jesus used innocent questions in a conversation as a means of building understanding and generating trust. The innocent question was part of life for Jesus and enabled him to create and develop rapport, empathy, and clarity.

The Absurd Question

Jesus seemed to delight in using questions to conjure up absurd situations as a means of encouraging the disciples and other individuals to reevaluate their thinking. Perhaps the best known of Jesus' absurd questions (which many people use without knowing its biblical origin) is, "Why do you look at the speck of sawdust in someone else's eye and pay no attention to the plank in your own eye?" (Matthew 7:3). Another absurd question, also found in the Sermon on the Mount, was, "If the salt loses its saltiness, how can it be made salty again?" (Matthew 5:13).

Jesus' use of the absurd question works superbly in terms of individuals seeing how their behavior can be interpreted as myopic or ridiculous. He employed this technique with powerful effect once his hearers were engaged with him.

The Question in Response to a Question

The classic example of this approach occurred when Jesus was asked whether or not taxes should be paid to Caesar (Mark 12:13–17). His first response was a question, "Why are you trying to trap me?" He then asked to see a coin and followed with another question, "Whose face and name are these?" After his hearers said it was the emperor's, Jesus responded with the statement, "Well, then pay the emperor what belongs to the emperor, and pay God what belongs to God."

Jesus used questions to draw out the real concerns of those with whom he spoke. He used questions to get to the root of their concerns and also as a means of not falling into the traps they were trying to set for him.

The Challenging Question

Jesus often took his disciples aside to explain to them the meaning of some of his teachings. He could be quite challenging with them, asking such questions as "Are your hearts hardened?" "Do you have eyes but fail to see?" and "Do you still not understand?"

Jesus had a remarkable ability to propel people into thinking in new ways. But his propensity to incite people was done in a purposeful way. With the disciples it was in the context of a relationship built up over some years together. With the Pharisees and other leaders it was his way of challenging them to break out of their rigid perspectives.

The Relevance of Jesus' Approach to Questioning Today

Examining the questions Jesus asked has reinforced to me the relevance of his approach in a range of spheres. Questions have been a key tool for me in different roles. For example, as a director general within the UK government—with a staff of over eight hundred people and in one role with responsibility for an expenditure of over forty billion pounds (eighty billion dollars)—I had to be able to ask questions that revealed inefficiencies and led to the best possible use of resources. When I write about leadership and spirituality, I need to understand the key questions in individuals' hearts as they take on bigger leadership roles. As a lay preacher, I need to understand the key questions in the minds of a congregation, and I will often begin a sermon with a question that I trust resonates with members of the congregation.

There are occasions when asking a question is not appropriate. Sometimes it is just being with someone—without asking questions—that matters. Questions are often best avoided with one's own children; they will tell us what they want to tell us at the time of their choosing! Questioning a recalcitrant teenager is probably the least effective way of building a relationship.

Sometimes you have to be careful that the hearer does not interpret a question as giving direction. Asking at the end of a discussion what action the individual proposes to take can ensure that the individual has reached his or her own conclusion rather than interpreting your question as giving direction.

It is worthwhile to ask yourself the following questions:
- How well do you use questions to build and grow relationships?
- Could you use questions more effectively, varying your repertoire more?
- Are there ways in which you could build into your repertoire the types of approaches Jesus used in his questioning?

Innocent Questions

The innocent, open-ended question is crucial for building relationships and acquiring a clear picture about a situation. If the questioner appears to take a particular perspective, that will influence the hearer's response. The most honest response will come in reply to an innocent question. As an executive coach, my main tool is an open-ended question that enables an individual to develop his or her own strategy for tackling a difficult issue. It is never right for me to impose a solution. Through the use of innocent questions I enable my client to work out a plan for his or her next steps.

I well remember a young, energetic Old Testament professor I had at Regent College in 1970. Carl Armerding had a great gift for posing questions about the book or text we were studying. The questions were always asked with an energy and positive approach that encouraged us to think through the issues and articulate clearly our level of understanding. Carl's knack for being both positive and searching in his use of questions served as a brilliant role model that I have tried to follow ever since.

Absurd Questions

The ability to describe or draw attention to the absurd in any situation can bring shared humor as well as a strong dose of reality. Questions that enable individuals to see the logical consequence of their behaviors or actions can be powerful. I might reframe the question "Is there a plank in your eye?" to "Are there ways in which you are blinded to reality?" I might ask a sequence of "What if?" questions that would enable an individual to take a particular set of actions to their logical conclusion in order to see if they ended in success or absurdity.

Questions in Response to a Question

In my role as an executive coach, I am often asked about my perspective based on my experience as a board member and as a director general within the UK government. Sometimes I will draw directly from my personal experience, but more often I will use my experience in order to ask follow-up questions that enable individuals to work out their own response to the problem with which they are dealing. When people develop their own answers to their questions, they are more likely to be committed to them than if they hear a canned answer that someone else provides.

The skill of asking the right supplementary question comes from being able to step inside the shoes of the questioner. As a coach, I spend a lot of time thinking about what it must be like to be in my clients' shoes. What issues and pressures are they facing? What options are they most likely to go for? Having stood in their shoes myself, I am in a better position to ask the supplementary questions that will enable them to move forward. For example, if their presenting question is about what their next step in their job should be, I may well respond by inviting them to think about questions such as "What gives you the greatest joy in your work?" "What is most fulfilling about your work?" "What next step would resonate best with your values?" or "Where do you want to be five years from now?"

Responding to a question with a question is often a great way of moving more deeply into understanding a difficult situation, provided there is a high level of quality engagement between those involved in the conversation.

Challenging Questions

By "challenging" questions, I do not mean haranguing questions. As soon as I feel that I am being lectured to, I turn the other person off. The preacher who tries to browbeat the hearer into submission is usually dismissed as someone who is not engaging with those to whom he is speaking.

A good challenging question goes to the heart of the matter and forces you to think. A successful challenging question takes account of the context. Ideally it is posed within a relationship where trust already exists and where the other party doesn't feel threatened by the tone of a challenging question. As a coach, I have found that there is no point in my asking a challenging question until I have built a strong rapport with the client. Then, once the ground rules are clear, a challenging question can help an individual develop a measure of resolve and courage to make difficult decisions that he or she had never conceived as possible before.

When I was a nonexecutive director of two major educational institutions, my job was to ask challenging questions. The nonexecutive brings a wider perspective and a clear responsibility to both support and challenge the executive leaders. In church life we are often surprisingly unwilling to be challenged by a fellow believer looking at the way we do things. Jesus challenged the religious and civic leaders of his day. We expect our schools, hospitals, and governmental organizations to be externally challenged. But sometimes we are reluctant to apply the same discipline to our Christian and church organizations.

Allow me to invite you to do the following:

- Observe those you know who ask questions well, noting how they do it and what sort of response they get.
- Reflect on how you use questions, noting when you use them well and when they provoke an unhelpful response.
- Reflect on the extent to which you could adopt some of the approaches Jesus used in asking questions.
- Consider whether you can more often ask innocent questions, absurd questions, questions in response to a question, and challenging questions.

Just as Jesus used questions effectively, the more we use questions in a well-planned and thoughtful way, the more influential we can be in the various contexts in which we live. Being influential is not to be measured in terms of imposing our views on others but rather in enabling them to become more effective leaders, teachers, citizens, and Christians.

GETTING THE BALANCE RIGHT

Getting the balance right might be viewed as acceding to a vague compromise. But getting the balance right is often what is needed to ensure success. Cyclists have to balance their weight precisely when going around a corner at a high speed. Skiers know that if they lose their balance they will lose their stability and end up rolling down the mountain.

The point of equilibrium may well be different for different people and vary depending on their stage of life. Seeking equilibrium is not about opting out; it is about getting as firm a basis as possible for making decisions and planning effectively for the future.

Christians face a wide range of issues related to balance. Several Christian leaders share their views in this regard in figure 9.

The comments in figure 9 illustrate the range of balancing acts with which Christian leaders wrestle. They seek to balance speed of delivery with the quality of what they bring. They champion truth and aim to be both principled and pragmatic.

Finding the right balance involves:
- frankness about what is important
- honesty about the facts, so that there is no sense of self-deception
- clarity about the objectives, including an acknowledgment if the objectives may be in potential conflict
- quiet reflection, so that emotional attitudes or past experiences do not distort
- prayerfulness, so that particular perspectives or decisions can be viewed in a wider context

Some key elements of balance with which the Christian leader wrestles include:
- ambition to lead versus a sense of service to others

Figure 9

GETTING THE BALANCE RIGHT

"Balancing personal and team success is important. It is making sure that the team gets credit for achieving the results, and not me. It is getting them to believe that the team's success is my success."—*private sector leader*

"As a military leader, you have to be clear what you are balancing. You have to identify what is nonnegotiable, and your people need to understand that well. On law or military discipline, there is no compromise: there are clear demarcation lines."—*military leader*

"Doing what is right involves a difficult balance. There are work pressures, but sometimes my parents are ill, and I need to spend time with them. The demand from these extremes can be a means of focus. I like to think my faith gives me a focus, but I do not always get the solutions right."—*management consultant*

"Doing deals can appear cutthroat. It takes time to build negotiating relationships and then lead by example. When doing deals, I try to stick to my core principles to ensure I get the balance right."—*private sector executive*

"I think it is a perpetual struggle. Responsibility leads to accountabilities. I took the view that outsourcing to India was contributing to a developing country. It is important to see the broad effects of globalization and recognize what is happening."—*HR director*

"You cannot impose your Christian values on other people. I carry the responsibility of knowing and believing that there is a right way to live, but I must respect that people come to decisions with a range of different values."—*HR director*

"In my leadership I have framed a servant leadership approach; my faith and its values lead me to place a large value on team rather than individual leadership."—*chief executive*

"Championing truth is important. But at the same time there is the art of the impossible and helping an organization get by. Enabling an organization to be better may inevitably be incremental."—*local government leader*

"It is important to be listening to people even when you have to make decisions quickly. You have to find the right balance between decisiveness and listening."—*chief executive*

"I struggle with the balance between responding to the needs for more expenditure and using taxpayers' money wisely. Bosses may have different views on working with people who have performance issues. How you reconcile these differences is important. I always try to articulate what I am doing and why, on the basis that people are more likely to respect me if I do that."—*finance director*

"There is often a required balance between quality of work and speed of work. It is balancing your own time against time pressures you put on others and stress you put on others."—*finance director*

"I would never compromise on principle, but I do talk to people about being pragmatic. I believe it is important to be pragmatic within a principled structure. Principles allow you to be more relaxed about being pragmatic. Pragmatism is not the opposite of principles. Sometimes it is saying this is what the rules say, but there does need to be a balance about the way we take this forward. Pragmatism is deciding which of the battles it is worth going for in terms of the overall ethical stance. You are not going to solve every problem straightaway. You have to be pragmatic in deciding what you are going to tackle first."—*private sector leader*

- developing your own skills versus enabling others to grow in effectiveness and responsibility
- building on your strengths versus developing your less strong areas
- focusing on the long term versus the short term
- providing enough financial resources for your family to live on while also making certain that there is adequate time and energy devoted to the lighter side of family life
- ensuring there is both serious intent and lighthearted spontaneity

The right balance point may not always be easily identified. It might vary depending on your age and circumstances. There will be moments when the dominant activity will be work or family or community or church. This might vary from one year to the next.

Keeping a sense of flexibility and growth is essential so that you do not become boxed in to a blinkered set of assumptions about the right balance. Jesus didn't go for a steady, predictable balance in the way he lived his life or mentored his disciples. There were plenty of surprises, activity, and energy for his disciples. No sooner had the people of Israel reached one point of balance when they were off on the next stage of their journey. The sense of pilgrimage that is part of Christian faith includes an acceptance that life is never static; the point of balance is forever changing.

Key questions to ask might be:
- What issues of balance are you currently facing?
- To what extent are these issues transitory because of your current context?
- What particular ways of using your time and energy do you want to reassess?

HANDLING RISKS WELL

Some of the key risks for a Christian in the secular world of work can include:

- being compromised on principles
- being captured by ambition
- being captivated by worldly success
- being fixated on financial aspirations
- becoming exhausted in a faster and faster world
- becoming too narrow minded about your vocation or career
- losing out on family time
- losing out on growing in Christian understanding
- losing out on contributing to Christian service
- not being nourished spiritually on a day-to-day basis
- being overwhelmed by emotional and physical needs

Comments from individual leaders on the risks they face as Christians are illustrated in figure 10.

The observations in figure 10 illustrate the variety of risks Christians face. Some risks are specifically related to an individual's particular job and circumstances. Others are generic and can result when a sense of purpose turns into inflated pride or the desire to be "in the world but not of the world" creates a duality that is difficult to navigate.

It is important to be honest about the risks you face and how you plan to address them. Pretending that risks don't exist leads to self-delusion and the heightening rather than the lowering of those risks and their consequences.

Helpful steps in addressing the risks that you face are to:

- know yourself well enough to understand the risks that are most pertinent to you
- recognize the circumstances that can lead to a particular risk coming to the fore
- know the early warning signals that reveal a problem that needs to be addressed

Figure 10

THE RISKS CHRISTIAN LEADERS FACE

"We can become worried about the accumulation of all the things we are doing. We need to be thankful for the breaks we have. We need to give ourselves time to have a break. You don't have to be a 10 at everything. You must not lose sight of the most important things. You have to have some time for yourself. You need to be continually growing as a Christian."—*management consultant*

"Family can be the big loser. Another is the risk of having an overinflated sense of importance. Hence I use an upside-down pyramid when I draw the hierarchy of management responsibilities. I know I do not spend enough time in quiet reflection. I go to a Saturday group of Christian leaders every six weeks, which provides a lot of support. Materialism is a risk, and I need to balance it. There is an issue of temptation and power in relation to people, which needs to be watched."—*chief executive*

"I believe my entire practical life is based on risk analysis. Every element of the plan has a risk analysis link to it. Time is my rarest asset. There is a danger of losing out on contributing to Christian service. I allocate time for both Christian reflection and service, in terms of meetings and reading on the train. Christian service is greatly helped through the encouragement of others. There is a big risk of not being nourished on a daily basis. It is too easy to get caught on a BlackBerry."—*private sector leader*

"A key risk is that faith can be 'condemned as irrelevant' because of the faults of some of the faithful. You just have to recognize that this is a fact."—*military leader*

"There is a great risk of duality. Christian service is seen as something you do at church and not what you do at work. There is a crucial seam of being holistic. It helps if those in your church understand you and the risks you are taking and your concerns."—*politician*

"There is a danger of Christians being put upon. Hence the importance of clarity about the use of time. Christians need to be encouraged to say gracefully what they cannot do."—*national politician*

"Not doing what God calls us to do. The sin of pride: the risk of believing that you are better than others."—*senior government official*

"Being in the world and not of it. A concern about living in a busy world is not nurturing your spirituality. It is important to see every moment as an act of prayer. You can be too preoccupied with day-to-day business."—*HR director*

"Time to do other things is crowded out, especially between career and families. There is a conscious tension between holding principles and being pragmatic. The danger is moving too much from principles to pragmatic values. We need to make sure that the pragmatic does not overrule principles. Key issues are the increased pressure on events—decisions having to be made quickly with electronic communication, meaning that decisions have to happen in real time."—*military leader*

"There is never enough time to communicate with God and my family. I can become fixated on financial aspirations and can then feel guilty about that. I am well rewarded. I can carry a huge guilt burden about my own achievement."—*private sector executive*

"The freneticism and drive of modern life. The self-pity theme can get in the way. The anonymity effect can mean that there is not a network of support."—*local authority leader*

"You can easily become frazzled. The family can lose out. Train journeys are invaluable for Bible reading. There is a balance between not being too heavenly minded while not being too focused in the world's eyes. This means watching that you are not too Christian for your own good. Soldiers will often coax it out of you. The question, 'What is a born-again Christian?' can be asked in a half-teasing way."—*military leader*

"People not buying into ethical standards or expectations. People who cut corners and play the office game. How best do you make a stand at work? You need something to measure standards against. It is how you deal with injustice that is important. There is a risk of not being confident to talk about these issues at work. Your belief in high standards can get squeezed out."—*finance director*

"Is your ambition for the sake of Christ, or is it worldly ambition? The biggest risk is conformity—letting behaviors around you rather than the Holy Spirit dominate how you behave. You can argue to yourself that this is right. Because we don't want to offend, there is a danger we may not challenge the norms when they need to be challenged."—*private sector leader*

"There is a risk of conforming to the expectations of another Christian as to how you should behave. A church can teach you to behave in a particular way, for example, 'You are a failure if you haven't shared your faith ten times a week.'"—*private sector leader*

"The media are waiting for you to make any sort of mistake. Being a police officer is a vocation. You aren't motivated by finances. But it is easy to make an error that can be captured by the newspapers. This can lead to risk aversion and not championing causes that could bring you into contact with the media."—*senior police leader*

"Being compromised on principles is an issue just as much for Christians as for those without a faith. It is easy to be taken in. The balance can be difficult: you will never get it absolutely right. My approach is based on the five Fs of faith, family, fitness, fun, and firm. That is the order of relevant importance, with *faith* first and *firm* last."—*private sector chief executive*

"When we are concerned about handling a particular risk, we will not be the first person to have addressed that risk. However isolated we feel sometimes, we are part of a wider heritage and community that has lived with these risks on a perpetual basis."—*private sector leader*

- be sure you have friends who will support you through different risks
- have a network of mentors and a coach who understand you well enough to enable you to reach the right conclusions on next steps
- be wary of people who will just preach at you or lecture you

Here are some questions to ask yourself in regard to each of the risks mentioned at the beginning of this section:

Being compromised on principles:
- How clear are you about the principles that are most important to you?
- When there is a risk of compromise, can you talk the issue through with a trusted colleague?
- To what extent does your organization recognize that there can be issues related to a conflict of principles?

Being captured by ambition:
- How honest are you with yourself about your level of ambition?
- Where your ambition is great, are you sure it is for the right reasons?
- To what extent is your ambition blinkered, and to what extent does it take account of changing circumstances and the views of people who are important to you?

Being captivated by worldly success:
- How important is recognition to you?
- Are you honest with yourself about what you would be prepared to sacrifice in order to reach the next level of status in your organization?
- What effect would losing your current status have on your well-being? How would you handle that if it happened?

Being fixated on financial aspirations:
- How important is it to you that your income progressively rises?

- What is the relationship between honest assessment of what you need to live on and your financial aspirations?
- How are you affected by seeing what others own?

Becoming exhausted in a faster and faster world:
- How would you assess yourself on your ability to pace your energy?
- How well do you understand what gives you energy and what saps your energy?
- When you begin to feel exhausted, do you have a coping strategy?

Becoming too narrow minded about your vocation or career:
- How often do you evaluate whether you are in the right area of work or activity?
- How open are you to a change in your vocation or career?

Losing out on family time:
- To what extent do you honestly think you have the balance right in this area?
- Are you clear what your bottom line is in terms of time and energy given to your family?
- How do you address difficulties and disappointments in your family?

Losing out on growing in Christian understanding:
- How much has your Christian understanding grown in the last year?
- In what areas would you like to study and reflect more?
- How do you best fortify yourself to think in new and creative ways?

Losing out on contributing to Christian service:
- What type of Christian service most thrills you?
- What more would you like to do in terms of Christian service?
- How can you best create the time and energy to make a greater contribution to Christian service?

Not being nourished spiritually on a day-to-day basis:
- What type of reading or prayer best nourishes you?
- How can you create space during the week, especially workdays, to provide a bit more room for personal nourishment and reflection?
- What person(s), through conversation and encouragement, helps you grow in wisdom and understanding?

Being overwhelmed by emotional and physical needs:
- How well do you understand your emotional and physical needs?
- How balanced is your life between meeting your vocational priorities while recognizing you also have emotional and physical needs to be met?
- How do you best cope with the inevitable tensions within you?

Part of our humanity is living with risks. If there were no risks, life would be boring, and we would not be growing in understanding and wisdom. But all these risks present huge challenges to us. Some of the risks will be greater for some people than others. Progress always comes through identifying risks, knowing ourselves well enough to understand how we respond, and having mechanisms in place that will enable us to handle risks as best we can.

Sometimes we can and should address a risk by completely avoiding an issue; for example, never going to a car showroom if there is a risk of wanting the status of a brand-new, expensive car. But sometimes it might be worth visiting the show room and smiling at our aspiration and then "parking" it and moving on!

THE VALUE OF MENTORING AND COACHING

Mentoring and coaching can play a crucial role in helping individuals address risks successfully. Many organizations encourage individuals to have a mentor. A business mentor is a veteran executive from the same or a similar business who has direct experience of the individual's broad situation and can help him or her work through different concerns effectively. The distinction between a mentor and a manager is that the mentor has no line management responsibility for the individual.

A mentor can provide a source of knowledge of the organization and its political climate, act as a sounding board for ideas, and help an individual think through and plan an overall career development path. For example, a procurement expert who has been through difficult procurement exercises can help mentor a newly qualified specialist. A prison warden who has talked with many prisoners and developed a sense of whether or not the inmates are telling the truth can help build up the same sensitivity in a younger prison officer. Similarly, a Christian who has been in a leadership role and knows the joys and pressures of such responsibilities can provide advice and a sounding board for the younger Christian leader.

The experience of the mentor and mentee need not be in precisely the same sector, but there does need to be some commonality about the leadership challenges that both have faced. A good mentor will ask questions in a way that enables an individual to develop his or her own thinking and understanding. The mentee, having worked out a strategy, can then use the mentor as a sounding board in judging whether the next steps are correct.

Focused external coaching can play an important part in enabling individuals to be effective leaders and balance risks well. In 2006, the partnership of which I am a member conducted an independent survey of eighty individuals whom we had coached. The individuals were asked about the objectives for the coaching, and they identified these four main types of objectives:

- *business issues:* strategic priorities, business planning, major projects
- *clarity of role:* transitional coaching into a new role, career

development, and preparation for subsequent roles

- *personal awareness*: personal impact, leadership style, self-confidence, and assertiveness
- *interpersonal skills*: influencing skills, stakeholder management, and team management and development

An external coach who has held a senior position in the private, public, or voluntary sector and has experience coaching people in a variety of situations can provide the external stimulus and challenge that can enable an individual to make difficult decisions well and become increasingly effective as a leader.

The benefits of one-to-one coaching with an experienced coach should be

- a healthier balance between personal and professional priorities;
- deeper self-confidence in tackling demanding challenges;
- greater courage in delivering change;
- a broader repertoire of approaches to solving problems;
- a clearer set of priorities;
- better use of time and energy;
- increased self-awareness and a better understanding of one's impact on others; and
- a clearer understanding of personal risks.

In regard to facing difficult decisions, the value of a coaching arrangement relates to the strengthening of the areas just mentioned as well as to the opportunity to use the coach as a sounding board in working through the decisions themselves.

The benefits for an organization that utilizes coaching for its senior leaders should include

- a clearer vision and strategy;
- a stronger commitment from leaders to organizational goals;
- a sharper set of priorities for the organization;

- stronger personal impact of the senior leaders both internally and externally;
- more productive working relationships;
- better delivery of results; and
- opportunities to test courses of action in a safe place.

The success of coaching in enabling individuals to lead and take risks well depends on

- the client's willingness to be honest about difficult personal and professional priorities;
- the quality of engagement between coach and client;
- the clarity of objectives for the coaching;
- the client's openness to change;
- the client's willingness to reflect and learn;
- the client's willingness to experiment with making difficult decisions and then embed that new learning;
- the accuracy of external feedback into the coaching discussions;
- the client's ability to use self-awareness constructively; and
- a recognition that coaching is a journey, requiring challenging objectives that evolve with experience.

Coaching, if it is to be effective, must be about focused conversations in which the client feels both firmly supported and effectively challenged and stretched. Good coaching will be both exhausting and invigorating. The long-term results will be a strong sense of purpose, a clarity about aspirations, and a set of pragmatic and focused next steps in addressing difficult issues. (In our book *Business Coaching: Achieving Practical Results through Effective Engagement*, Robin Linnecar and I set out in more detail the impact of coaching, what makes a good coach, different formats for coaching, and different contexts where coaching can make a significant difference.)

Alastair Redfern, the bishop of Derby, England, worked with a coach during his initial two years as bishop. Here are some comments he wrote during that time:

> The coaching helps me step back away from the job. Working with an external coach provides the additional distance, which means that I can reflect more dispassionately about what I am doing than in conversations with anybody else. The coach brings their experience in management and leadership in very different organisations. In our conversations, we break down some of the issues and then put them back together again in a way that helps me decide on next steps. The coach gives me the type of questions but it is very much up to me to reach the conclusions. He never tells me what to do but enables me to think issues through.
>
> In the coaching conversations, the coach listens a lot, he helps me interpret some of the issues and enables me to articulate some of the strategic next steps. He brings a very different frame of reference. The conversations are always enjoyable, engaging and stretching. They help me look at things in new ways. I go out energised by the process and I look forward to the coaching conversations. I am always forced to think hard and come out of the conversations clearer in my own mind about my next steps.[9]

For Alastair, the coaching conversations involved hard thinking and a discipline of crystallizing practical next steps. The opportunity to stand back and reflect with someone with a different perspective can be a powerful benefit of coaching.

---

9.   Peter Shaw and Robin Linnecar, *Business Coaching: Achieving Practical Results through Effective Engagement* (Chichester, UK: Capstone, 2007), 72.

In *Business Coaching*, Robin Linnecar and I talk about the "golden thread" running through effective engagement between coach and client.

Figure 11

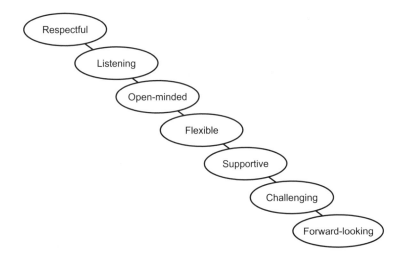

Being *respectful* involves trust and unconditional mutual regard. *Listening* requires being fully present and giving the other person your sole and undivided attention. Being *open-minded* is about banishing preconceived notions, being fully attentive to the client's agenda, and finding the point of need. Being *flexible* calls for varying the approach, pace, and timing to fit the circumstances of the individual, using a variety of models. Being *supportive* is about encouragement, emphasizing the positive and helping individuals keep up their energy. Being *challenging* has to do with an engagement between equals where the coach is not too deferential: it is about slicing through the dross and holding up a mirror to the client. Being *forward-looking* means having a relentless focus on the future, whatever past or current travails there have been.

We suggest there are four levels of engagement between coach and client.

Figure 12

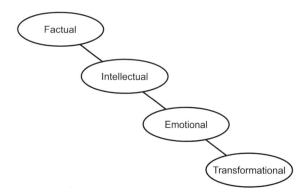

Factual is about being on the same page in terms of information. It means having a significant understanding of the background and the context. It doesn't require an encyclopedic knowledge of an area, but it does involve a good understanding of the key limits and issues.

Intellectual involves being able to talk about issues on equal terms in a robust way; it includes seeing the policy and operational consequences of different actions.

Emotional has to do with creating relationships whereby clients are willing to be open about their emotional reactions and to move on, through recognizing what they find difficult and how they want to develop their own capacity for courage and resilience. Emotional reactions from others may be getting in the way of a client's clear, authentic leadership. If the coach can help bring clarity, a roadblock to progress can be removed.

Transformational pertains to a quality of coaching discourse that results in clients viewing themselves and their situation in an entirely different way. The coach has to be prepared to read his or her own emotional reactions in a coaching discussion, using them as a barometer of the impact the client has on others.

In the best of coaching discussions there is the creativity of two people working well together. There is focused questioning and dialogue in which the overall result is more than the sum of the parts. The interaction leads to creative and dynamic progress toward new solutions. When the coach and client look back, they are often surprised by the progress that has taken place.

As a professional coach, I work with people of faith as well as individuals with no faith. The levels of engagement set out above are equally appropriate in either case. When clients are explicit about their Christian faith and understanding, it does allow for an additional dimension in the coaching. We are able to tackle, in a holistic way, the interrelationship between their faith and work perspectives—underpinned by realism about their hopes and aspirations and an acceptance that they are seeking to live out God's will in the world and fulfill their sense of Christian service and vocation.

ENSURING EFFECTIVE FEEDBACK

Good feedback is a precious gift to give someone, provided it is done in a way that encourages that person to move on constructively. Feedback that is critical and insensitive can be damaging, as we all know. Jesus gave his disciples feedback, although they were not always quick to learn. Sometimes he gave the feedback in a direct way: "Why could you not stay awake?" But his feedback was always given within a quality of relationship, which meant that it was accepted and acted upon.

Feedback is never to be given lightly or wantonly. Sometimes an 80:20 rule applies, whereby the feedback needs to be 80 percent positive so that the other 20 percent will be properly accepted and taken forward. Part of "loving your neighbor as yourself" is being honest in feedback. Genuine love is enabling others to grow and develop so that they can become more fully the people God created them to be.

Key questions to ask yourself in terms of your own reception of feedback might be:

- How do you respond to feedback? Do you become defensive, or do you accept feedback with a positive attitude?
- From whom do you best receive feedback? How do you create situations whereby that person(s) will give you feedback in an honest, constructive, and supportive way?
- How do you decide what aspects of feedback to act upon and when to say, after hearing the feedback, that you are going to continue in a similar vein?
- How do you let people know that you have reflected on the feedback they have given and have been deliberate in your next steps?

In terms of giving feedback to others:

- How receptive are you when people want feedback from you?
- How do you approach a situation in which an individual is reluctant to receive feedback but does need to reflect on the impact he or she is having on others?
- What is the best way to give feedback to people so that they feel you are making a positive rather than a negative contribution?
- How willing and prepared are you to make sure there is mutuality in the giving and receiving of feedback?

ATTRIBUTES TO AVOID

Figure 13 sets out the comments of individual leaders regarding attributes that Christians need to avoid.

Figure 13

ATTRIBUTES TO AVOID AS A CHRISTIAN

"Inconsistency, hypocrisy, saying one thing and doing another, giving a false prospectus."—*management consultant*

"Untrustworthiness, appearing to blame others."—*private sector leader*

"Being sanctimonious."—*senior government official*

"Hypocrisy."—*HR director*

"Self-serving."—*private sector executive*

"Being a bit of a fraud; things don't add up. Hiding behind the veneer of Christianity. Not being interested in people, as the task is more important. Not appearing to listen."—*military leader*

"Conformity. Letting the standards and behaviors around you dominate how you behave, rather than the Holy Spirit."—*international management consultant*

"Those who present themselves as religious but then use it as a smoke screen to hide what is being done."—*finance director*

"Inconsistency between belief and behavior. People will try to find an element of hypocrisy to hang their disbelief on. It is important to be aware that the disciples learned from Jesus every day. We are on a journey. The way we do what we do will make the impact. Consistency is important."—*private sector executive*

"You must not have a hidden agenda. I aim to be as transparent as I can be. You have to be discreet and not play out an agenda. I don't want to be perceived to be doing things for the wrong reasons."—*senior police leader*

"Duplicity and untrustworthiness are the most uncomfortable words. I am less uncomfortable with failure to deliver. Subversive activity is something I would not want to be known by. There is a danger of being branded 'holier than thou.' You have to watch being accused of only understanding black and white."—*senior international banker*

"You have to watch greed, misleading people, lack of trust, and lack of authenticity."—*chief executive*

"Things to avoid include being untrustworthy, hypocrisy, duplicity, failure to deliver, setting out a false prospectus, financial irresponsibility, bullying, manipulating, subversive activity, unnecessary confrontation, blaming others, hiding problems, and bigotry."—*private sector leader*

"Incompetence."—*senior lawyer*

These comments make for disturbing reading. None of us want to be branded as untrustworthy, unreliable, inconsistent, sanctimonious, incompetent, duplicitous, or manipulative. If we are regarded as possessing any of these attributes, our tendency may be to feel misunderstood or misinterpreted. We can view ourselves as martyrs or persecuted or suffering for our faith, though we have caused the problems in the first place! Jesus' words about being concerned about the speck in someone else's eye when there is a log in our own are relevant here.

If colleagues or critics do use the adjectives in the previous paragraph about us, we need to determine if there is an element of truth in the observation. And if so, we must be clear about how we move forward in order to become less subject to such criticism.

How do we avoid being associated with the attributes listed above? Practical steps might include:

- Be clear on your priorities so that the risk of making inconsistent decisions is minimized.
- Hold firmly to key principles that are touchstones of the way you respond to particular situations.
- Ensure that you have enough feedback from those you trust so that you are well informed about whether any of your attitudes or behaviors can be misinterpreted.
- In order to minimize the risk of inconsistency in a particular situation, give yourself enough space to be able to reflect before responding.
- State explicitly what the stakes in the ground that are important to you are, so that the chances of misrepresentation are kept to a minimum.

What if you get feedback that you are being associated with one of the attributes to avoid? Here is a checklist to consider:

- Is there any factual basis for this view?
- How widely shared is this view?
- How do your most trusted colleagues regard the situation? Do they see this assessment of you as completely unjustified?
- Would it be appropriate to try to talk in an open and frank way with the individuals concerned regarding their perspective?
- What practical steps can you take to demonstrate that you believe and act in a way that is opposite to this negative attribute?

If you become aware that you are being identified with a negative attribute, being depressed, irritated, or cross about it is rarely going to help. Staying as dispassionate as possible will help keep your emotional reaction consistent with what, in your rational moments, you think you ought to do. But there will be a need to let go of your emotions. Here is where a conversation with good friends, sharing in a church or group situation, and praying intently about the issue can be so helpful.

If you become consumed by such an issue, reflect on what will help you break through. It might be a Scripture verse that is precious to you or reminding yourself of some words of wisdom from a Christian writer or friend. It might be the words of a hymn or song that ring in your ear. The key is to hold on to what is good and true and not let any sense of rumor or manipulation by others undermine your faith or your confidence as you live in God's sight.

Some Christians would say that if we aren't being persecuted, then we aren't being explicit enough about our faith. There will be some occasions and some organizations where Christians will be criticized or ostracized because of the views they express, particularly when they stand up to support standards of behavior or morality that many people are ignoring. When this happens, these individuals need our support and encouragement. We need to be careful, however, not to regard a certain amount of teasing as persecution. We can take some occasional remarks out of proportion and feel we are being criticized or persecuted. The danger then is that we see being "persecuted" as a virtue and give up on trying to communicate with our colleagues. It is quite possible to share a good working relationship with them and to impact them through our faith and personal values.

LIVING WITH OUR IMPERFECTIONS

Sometimes the attributes we wish to avoid are rightly used to describe us. Living with our imperfections is part of life. We grow when we are aware of our mistakes and are willing to forgive ourselves. If forgiving others is tough, forgiving ourselves can be in another league altogether. In the words of C. S. Lewis, "Everyone says forgiveness is a lovely idea, until they have something to forgive."

Living with our imperfections requires avoiding being too driven, being comfortable in our skin, and recognizing that we don't always get the balance of life right. Addressing these themes actively involves

- being honest with ourselves, our family, our friends, and God;
- accepting the fact that we need to live with human frailties and vulnerabilities;
- recognizing how we best rise to becoming the kind of person we want to be rather than the kind of person we are in danger of becoming;
- being able to laugh at ourselves when we don't get the balance right; and
- ensuring that there are good friends and support groups around us who can encourage us and enable us to give our best, no matter what.

Failure and disappointment are part of working life. We strive so hard to reach a particular objective, but then the objective changes or the priorities become entirely different. Because of economic changes, an approach that was successful one week can be doomed to failure the next.

Failure and disappointment provide an opportunity to grow. In his book *God at Work: Living Every Day with Purpose*, Ken Costa emphasizes the importance of dealing with the chain of negative emotions that can be set off by a perceived failure. "Failure is like a train that pulls behind it a coach of disappointment and linked to that a coach of self-pity, and then a coach of rejection, and then another coach of 'I've had enough,' and finally a coach of all-pervading pessimism."[10]

Costa speaks of the danger, following a peak of work, of being left with a clear schedule but no adrenaline, wondering what you could have

---

10. Ken Costa, *God at Work: Living Every Day with Purpose* (London: Continuum, 2007), 144.

done better. He wrote: "Living each day at work with hope and purpose is essential for our well-being. It is true that those who are purpose-led have a positive outlook on life and produce better results both at work and outside it, influencing the communities in which they live. So, it is important to recover hope when, through failure and disappointment, we have lost its power to keep us expectant."[11]

Costa shares five pointers that he finds helpful when trying to recover from disappointment:

- Turn to God; take the initiative to lift your head toward him. As we do so, we are reminded of Christ's love for us, his victory on the cross, and the power of his resurrection.
- Face the facts; bring realism to bear when you deal with disappointments. When we contend with our discouragements, we need to avoid fantasies and daydreams of what might have been. There is no value in an indulgent reconstruction of the past.
- Meditate on Scripture; find God's promises in the Bible that are appropriate to your situation. By his creative Holy Spirit, God enables us to grow in hope—breaking the bounds of our narrowness.
- Keep a journal, as this enables you to articulate your thoughts and feelings. Written words seem to have a more objective ring to them than spoken words.
- Persevere in hope, recognizing that character is developed by learning to live in the midst of disappointment and by recovering hope for the long term. Christian hope is dynamic and powerful, whereas disappointment tends to constrict us, reducing our motivation and contracting our horizons.[12]

---

11. Ibid., 148.
12. Ibid., 148–151.

Strengthening our ability to cope with failure will create a resilience within us that will benefit us during future difficult times. Key points to reflect on might be:

- What effect did previous failures have upon you, and how were you able to move on from your sense of failure?
- What are the risks of failure for you currently, and how prepared are you to respond to those risks?
- How do you react when you see others experiencing failure? How can you best respond to their situation in a way that will enable them to live more effectively with their predicament?
- What can you do to be better prepared to cope with future failure, especially those failures that are unpredictable?

Failure is frequently clear cut and obvious. Disappointment can be much more insidious. Our family and friends often do not see why we are disappointed. What they see is life flowing forward in a reasonably ordered way. Disappointment can be very personal and affect our emotional sense of well-being or fulfillment.

Jesus experienced a sense of disappointment with his disciples. Peter's threefold denial surely came with the blow of being let down by a member of Jesus' inner circle. Jesus kept the focus on what was most important in his ministry, even though there must have been a strong element of sadness about the limited learning of his disciples.

How do we best cope with disappointment? Possible steps are:

- Remember how you have coped with disappointments in the past and moved on successfully.
- Consider what good might come out of this particular disappointment.
- Reflect on what you are learning about yourself and those around you as a consequence of this disappointment.
- Ask yourself how this disappointment might help you clarify your own next steps.

One senior leader in the private sector gave this advice to those building their careers and living through success and disappointment:

- Do not be afraid of new challenges and opportunities.
- Develop an ability to let go, and don't believe that conformity to your current surroundings is crucial.
- Do not be afraid of success; embrace it, but always remember the importance of people.
- Pray into your work situation, covering the people, the context, and the working environment.

LIVING THE BEATITUDES

Now when Jesus saw the crowds, he went up on a mountainside and sat down. His disciples came to him, and he began to teach them.

He said:

"Blessed are the poor in spirit,

for theirs is the kingdom of heaven.

Blessed are those who mourn,

for they will be comforted.

Blessed are the meek,

for they will inherit the earth.

Blessed are those who hunger and thirst for righteousness,

for they will be filled.

Blessed are the merciful,

for they will be shown mercy.

Blessed are the pure in heart,

for they will see God.

Blessed are the peacemakers,

for they will be called children of God.

Blessed are those who are persecuted because of

righteousness,

for theirs is the kingdom of heaven.

Blessed are you when people insult you, persecute you
and falsely say all kinds of evil against you because of
me. Rejoice and be glad, because great is your reward
in heaven, for in the same way they persecuted the
prophets who were before you."—Matthew 5:1–12

The Sermon on the Mount presents Jesus as much more than another lawgiver. The Beatitudes outline the attitudes of true disciples. Dick France, in his commentary on Matthew's Gospel, notes that the rewards of discipleship are spelled out in the second half of each verse, with the emphasis on the certainty that discipleship will not be in vain.[13]

Tom Wright comments that if we think of Jesus just sitting there telling people how to behave properly we will miss what was really going on.

These "blessings," the "wonderful news" that he's announcing, are not saying "try hard to live like this." They are saying that the people who already are like that are in good shape. They should be happy and celebrate.

Jesus is not suggesting that these are simply timeless truths about the way the world is, about human behaviour. If he was saying that, he was wrong. Mourners often go uncomforted, the meek don't inherit the earth, those who long for justice frequently take that longing to the grave. This is an upside-down world, or perhaps a right-way-up world; and Jesus is saying that with his work it's starting to come true. This is an announcement, not a philosophical analysis of the world. It's about something that is starting to happen, not about a general truth of life. It is gospel: good news, not good advice.[14]

---

13. R. T. France, *Matthew* (Leicester, UK: Inter-Varsity, 1985), 107–8.
14. Tom Wright, *Matthew for Everyone: Part 1: Chapters 1–15* (London: SPCK Publishing, 2002), 36.

The challenge is that we are to be the means whereby

- the poor in spirit begin to share in the kingdom of heaven;
- those who mourn are comforted;
- those who are meek begin to inherit the earth;
- those who hunger and thirst for righteousness will be filled;
- those who are merciful will be shown mercy;
- those who are pure in heart will see God;
- those who are peacemakers are recognized as the children of God; and
- those who are persecuted know they are part of the kingdom of God.

The resonant phrases of the Beatitudes may flow over us like water off a duck's back, but they can be such a source of inspiration as we reflect on them in light of the part we can play in enabling God to work and speak through us as we participate in bringing the kingdom of God to others.

Wright observes, "This list of 'wonderful news' is part of his invitation, part of his way of saying that God is at work in a fresh way and that this is what it looks like. Jesus is beginning a new era for God's people and God's world. From here on, all the controls people thought they knew about are going to work the other way round. In our world, still, most people think that wonderful news consists of success, wealth, long life, victory in battle. Jesus is offering wonderful news for the humble, the poor, the mourners and the peacemakers."[15]

Our challenge as Christians in the workplace is to bring a reflective approach so that the normally accepted measures of success might be turned on their heads. We are to nurture the poor in spirit, encourage those who are mourning, develop those who are meek, reinforce those who are striving to do what is right, inspire those who are willing to

---

15. Ibid.

be merciful toward those who have made mistakes, affirm those who are pure in heart, commend those who bring peace and harmony, and support those who feel persecuted in the workplace.

The call of the Beatitudes is not to be weak and softhearted, but to recognize the good in people and to develop them irrespective of their history, their vulnerabilities, and their level within the organization. We need to respect people for who they are as individuals, not for their status or wealth.

Key questions to ask might be:
- Who in your organization do you view as blessed? Who would you like to see blessed?
- How can you recognize those who are poor in spirit or meek or in need of mercy, especially when their needs may be largely hidden?
- How much do you help others to rejoice and be glad, whether or not they feel blessed within the organization?
- How might you reflect on each beatitude and let it infuse your way of thinking and acting even more?

CONCLUSION

In this third section we have looked at the importance of a Christian leader being reflective. We have started with Christian character, we have considered listening and engaging effectively, we have seen the heart of leadership as asking the right questions, we have thought about getting the balance of life right, we have reflected on handling risks well, we have looked at the value of mentoring and coaching, we have noted the value of ensuring effective feedback, we have thought about personal attributes to avoid and about living with our imperfections. We have seen living the Beatitudes as central to bringing a reflective approach within the workplace.

Some final reflections:
- Reflect on what Christian character means.

- Work hard at listening and engaging effectively.
- Consider what are the best open-ended questions to ask in order to draw out from others the right way ahead for them.
- Be willing to think hard about what is the right balance of life for you at this stage.
- Be honest about the risks you face and how you can best handle them.
- Always take the opportunities that are available to receive mentoring and coaching.
- Ensure that you have the best possible sources of feedback and are conscious of the attributes you want to avoid and how best to live with your own imperfections.
- Let the well-known words of the Beatitudes flow through your heart and your mind so that you can continuously reappraise and embed what is most important to you.

Above all, take time to reflect. Don't rush around trying to sort out all the problems and challenges at the same time. Just as Jesus found time to be reflective, allow yourself to step back in order that you can be both fully absorbed in your work and the other aspects of your life and refreshed and renewed by God's love and grace.

RENEWED

Being renewed is not a case of infrequent supercharging. It is an ongoing process whereby we look up rather than down, view our lives as half full rather than half empty, and remain open to the prompting and leading of the Holy Spirit. We keep being renewed through learning from the experience of others, receiving support from the Christian communities of which we are a part, and creating space to think, reflect, and pray. We are renewed as we relive the biblical narrative and experience the Scriptures on a regular basis. We are renewed as we think about our vocation and the future use of our time and energy. Renewal includes being ready to be surprised, being willing to step out confidently on the next steps of our personal journey. It means living life to the full while being upheld by the richness of God's love.

WHY DO WE NEED TO KEEP BEING RENEWED?

A battery that is not recharged eventually goes dead. A person who does not rest becomes exhausted and of no use to anyone. A battery can be recharged in different ways, depending on the way it is constituted. A human being is renewed through a variety of different contexts that transform an individual's physical, intellectual, emotional, and spiritual well-being. Paul enjoined the Romans: "Do not conform to the pattern of this world, but be transformed by the renewing of your mind. Then you will be able to test and approve what God's will is—his good, pleasing and perfect will" (Romans 12:2).

In 2 Corinthians 4, Paul wrote about our present weakness in light of resurrection life. He stated, "Therefore we do not lose heart. Though outwardly we are wasting away, yet inwardly we are being renewed day by day. For our light and momentary troubles are achieving for us an eternal glory that far outweighs them all. So we fix our eyes not on what is seen, but on what is unseen, since what is seen is temporary, but what is unseen is eternal" (2 Corinthians 4:16–18). We experience a continuous process of renewal as we fix our eyes on what is eternal. Renewal is available to us on a daily basis as we address the issues of each day. Renewal comes from a combination of focusing on an eternal God and not losing heart.

Learning from the Experiences of Others

In this section, four leaders share aspects of their leadership journey. They are Matthew Frost, the chief executive of Tearfund, a Christian relief and development organization; Matt Baggott, the chief constable of the Northern Ireland police force; Stephen Bampfylde, the chief executive of Saxton Bampfylde, a headhunting organization working at very senior levels; and Roger, who is a Christian leader in the business world. I encourage you to consider the relevance of their perspectives for your own experience.

Matthew Frost

The Christian leader brings both a soft side and a steely inner core, both humility and fierce resolve. Christ-centered living leads both to brokenness and to a powerful sense of purpose and calling founded on a recognition that we are beloved of God.

Christian leaders head purposefully toward God's purpose for their lives, a single beacon on the horizon. They ask, "How am I living in God's framing story, and what is my role within it?"

When I reflected on my calling, my purpose, a key issue for me was "What is my 'holy discontent'? Where does my God-given passion intersect with the service of people? How in all this will I love my neighbor?"

We should wrestle with God about what to do. I need to be ready to say, "Here I am; your servant is listening." Reflecting on what we are good at, what we love doing, is important. Sometimes the pull is in more than one direction. Finding our calling, our purpose, involves co-creation, not sitting and waiting. As we move—try things out—God steers and guides us. Our next step may well be about doing the obvious thing, pushing on the presenting door. Our calling may well not be so much about choosing issues but about choosing a community of people, and then the issues will choose you. Throughout, prayer is key.

There is a purpose that God wants to bless, and it is vital that the Christian leader find out what it is. This calling will entail wholehearted engagement in the world. It will be something I am passionate about. It will lead to serving others, to loving my neighbor. And as I begin to pursue my God-given calling, I find I do so wholeheartedly, single-mindedly, and with a fierce resolve to do as best I am able, as God has asked.

I am passionate about Tearfund's vision to see local churches transforming the lives of people in poverty through word and deed, in the Spirit. It takes my breath away when I see small local churches in the slums of India, gathered under no more than a tarpaulin, loving the poorest in their own communities, meeting their physical, emotional, and spiritual needs.

It's critical to my leadership role that I keep people both inside and outside Tearfund focused on this vision. I share stories whenever I can from our frontline in order to keep the vision vibrant and clear.

The words "Blessed are the poor in spirit" speak to me of brokenness as an amazing gift. I am broken yet redeemed; I am broken and loved. Brokenness leads to humility, which leads to learning, and then to the recognition that I do have a role to play in God's scheme of things. We need enough confidence to enable us to be humble.

When I was offered this job, I was upfront about my strengths and weaknesses. I wanted the appointing panel to have all the information on the table. Authentic leadership implies being clear and transparent about our strengths and weaknesses. It demands a hunger to receive feedback, both positive and negative. My brokenness drives me to seek God's wisdom, leading, and guidance—doing things in his strength, not my own.

I am finding that listening is a crucial attribute of the Christian leader. A week before I took the job at Tearfund, the burden of responsibility that came with it weighed heavily on me. I felt pretty low. But during my reflection and prayer time I came away with a very clear message. I understood God to say, simply, "You do not have to carry the responsibility—what I want you to do is to listen to others and to listen to me."

The first few months on the job were all about listening and learning, followed by playing back the key themes to staff. From then on the way forward became very clear. Since then I have tried to make it my first priority to give enough unhurried, agenda-free time to listen to God and to listen to colleagues and those we serve who live in poverty. For the last three years I have set aside three hours on Friday afternoons to journal, listen to God, pray, and reflect. Without this time I do not think I could cope with the pressures of the job. I also try to prioritize another couple of hours a week simply to chat with colleagues in the building, hearing what's on their minds.

I am task orientated, love solving problems, and can be impatient. At times I get totally immersed in driving an agenda and focusing on performance. So listening often goes against my grain. It's a skill I'm still learning to master. I have to work hard to resist the temptation to solve others people's problems, to step in and fix things. As I listen to those I lead I discover their strengths and weaknesses, their passion, their gifts, their concerns. I learn from them, receive feedback from them. I can pray for them. And I can help them get on to God's agenda and to be true to their own calling.

This emphasis on listening helps us create a high-performing leadership team. Our debate is more open, vulnerable, and direct. Trust is deepening. We play to each other's strengths and weaknesses. We empathize with each other. We problem-solve more effectively. We use a "team barometer" to gauge how we think we are performing. We try to give frequent, one-to-one, direct feedback to each other.

There is no shortage of risks for me as a leader. Work pressure threatens to crowd out unhurried time with God and with colleagues. I drift into thinking I have the answers and I can do this all in my own strength. Under pressure I stop listening to my colleagues and simply direct and solve other people's issues myself. I allow my own role to drift into areas that should remain the responsibility of others. Pride can creep in as I exaggerate my own importance and contribution.

I am convinced that Christian leadership is rooted above all else in a relationship with God. Deepening my relationship with God is the single most helpful, the single most important thing I can do as the leader of Tearfund.

Matthew is in a role that brings together his leadership experience in government and in a management consultancy prior to becoming chief executive of an aid organization. Matthew brings complete honesty about the joys and apprehension of leadership, and he has a keen willingness to see his role as part of God's story of bringing practical development aid. He wrestles with the balance of time and energy between competing priorities. He deliberately takes time out to reflect and pray as a means of keeping each of the different aspects in harmony.

Questions to ask yourself based on Matthew's experience might be:

- Where does brokenness fit in for you in terms of recognizing your own humanity and limitations and at the same time responding to leadership pressures and expectations?
- Do you resonate with Matthew's focus on the importance of listening? What steps might you take as a result?

Matt Baggott

As a teenager, I believed it was my calling to join the police force. This was strongly confirmed in my first posting; the inspector in charge had prayed for a Christian to join him! And I have never wavered in this sense of calling.

I was an inspector at age twenty-five and was running a riot squad, which was incredibly reactive. Then I went to university and studied history, where the theme was less of the microscope and more of the telescope. When I went back to Brixton, everything was thrown at me: murder, robbery, and child murder. Initially I thought, *What am I doing here?* The Holy Spirit was churning it up. The Lord gave me strength to see my way through it. I was challenged: *Are you really prepared to live the gospel?* After two months I was asked to take responsibility for half of Brixton and given the opportunity to see Brixton through the telescope, not the microscope, and to make long-term changes in approach.

We needed to focus on relationship building at the housing estates. We spent time talking and gaining trust. This led to information and support to free the areas from criminal oppression. This led to a huge transformation. The key themes were guardianship and social justice. We were there to transform people's lives. Suddenly I realized I had a calling to a ministry of social healing. We worked closely with the church in Brixton. The outcome was to rekindle some sort of social mission within the church, which had become disconnected from the local communities. The police became the catalyst for positive change.

I worked with a group of thoughtful people in Brixton who were thinking about different ways of policing inner-city areas. Since then, God has provided a myriad of opportunities to influence social transformation, both locally and nationally. I went to the Metropolitan Police Service headquarters to develop social/policing policy and to Peckham, working on social transformation alongside the government. Then I went to the West Midlands police force, where we redesigned the way we looked at neighborhood renewal and social justice. What has influenced me over the years is learning to be more reflective and disciplined; trying to discern God's heart for me and letting that shape my direction; becoming more relaxed; and believing that if God wants something to happen, it will. At the same time, you have to be at the top of your game professionally.

What gets in the way? A Christian colleague came to see me, bringing a set of brass scales as a message from the Lord. The message was that I had gotten the balance wrong. My job had become too important to me. I needed to reflect on the importance of time for self, for family, and for God. It was time to revisit how I could best follow God's will. God wants us to enjoy life and find the right balance. I was incredibly reassured. There was a sense of God shaping me for eternity. You are there to be a rounded Christian.

It is important that you go about leading in the right way. Social transformation is important. You need to lead by example. You need to be clear about what, as a leader, you are going to focus on. You get into discussions with colleagues about what should happen next; you pool mutuality and not imposition. Servant leadership is about trying to see issues through the eyes of other people.

From the leadership of Jesus, I see clarity of purpose and a readiness to be submissive to what is right. He was prepared to go through the agony before the crucifixion. He was not deflected. He was submissive to God's calling. The way he loved and forgave people was crucial. He built his church on flawed people. Jesus kept rebuilding his people.

As a leader, there needs to be generosity in seeing the best in people. You can't start with suspicion. You have to trust. You must have fairness and integrity, alongside compassion. Key risks are avoiding the issue and not confronting dilemmas. Are you tackling the problem and doing it with thoughtfulness and integrity? Can you justify what you are doing?

The real world of Christian discipleship is at the sharp end. It is working with the victim who is bleeding. It is addressing the criminal who is getting away with it. One individual once gave me a painful kicking, but I knew that restraint rather than retribution was the right response. God confirmed this when the fellow wrote to me and apologized!

As a Christian leader, it is important to ask questions about why you are where you are. You need to rise above some of the detail and disagreements. You need to keep focusing on the mission and not be deflected.

When making hard decisions, I try to reflect on what needs to be resolved. I try to find time to put the decision before the Lord. It is important that I do not close off the Holy Spirit. Leadership is about being professional in getting the right people around the table. It is encouraging honesty and plain speaking. It is acknowledging that I am frail.

It is important to find time for worship and study. You can become closed to the Lord in simply being too busy. And there

is a danger of focusing your life on work issues rather than the
first steps of your children or grandchildren.

When you fail, remember that God forgives you, honors you,
and picks you back up. The God of the universe is the God who
directs your life. He lives within you. Trust the Lord; don't hang
on to things that will deflect you. Trust God's unfailing love.

When you face major issues, it is important to remember the
theme of submission to God. Realize that God sees into your
heart and wants humility on your part as well as to use your
gifts. You have to be on guard against busyness crowding out
important things, a danger in days when you do not have time
to reflect. Define what is important, and remember to put the
stones, not the sand, into the jar first.

What Matt most enjoys about his work is seeing people's lives being turned around, helping to create an organization that brings about
change in society, and seeing people discover their own self-confidence.
He wants to see people of balance: individuals who recharge their batter-
ies, individuals who are active but also read books and go fishing!

Some of the key themes that flow from Matt's story are:

- the energy that flows from addressing issues of social justice
- the continuous learning of a leader in rapidly changing
  situations
- the language of discerning God's heart for you

As you think about Matt's journey, some questions to reflect on
might be:

- How might your leadership contribution be bringing social
  justice?
- How do you balance the adrenaline flow of a busy job with
  the need for relaxation and reflection?
- How does the language of "not clos[ing] off the Holy Spirit"
  impact what might seem to be a very secular leadership role?

Stephen Bampfylde

As a Christian leader, I bring Christian love and advice. I do not hide my Christian faith. On our organization's twenty-second birthday, a number of us (one-third of the total staff) went to Westminster Abbey for Communion. We live life looking forward, choosing the people and organizations we work with. I want to live a seamless life. I don't want a distinction between faith, life, and work. It helps that my cofounder had the same views. We both found that Alton Abbey, an Anglican Benedictine community, became part of our lives.

We use the Rule of Saint Benedict as a management primer. We talk about our receptionist as the gatekeeper, taking her job description from the one Benedict provides for the abbey gatekeeper. She is just as much part of the team as anybody else. We stole the chapter house concept from the Rule of Saint Benedict: if you have been at the firm for two years or more, you are part of the council, which is a nonhierarchical body and the center of the organization. We talk, in this council, about living the values of the firm. We measure this once a year and track it over time.

Jesus met people where they were. He was open and consistent. Jesus was available some of the time but not all of the time. The concept of servant leadership is important. Going to Alton Abbey on a regular basis is important to me because it puts things into perspective. Sometimes there is too much of a "Christian nice guy" in me. Christ was capable of being tough, and sometimes that is essential in leaders.

Setting out those standards to clients and other individuals is important. Honesty, which means telling colleagues the true picture, is important. Excellence is necessary. I need to allow space so people can develop their talents. One individual wanted to become a psychotherapist, so we enabled her to work three days a week and do her psychotherapy training the other two days. We created a situation where she could develop her talents.

I have been taken advantage of at times. I would rather be trusting and believe in individual goodness, but you never know if you will get it quite right. There is a risk of becoming too worldly. The joy of being in business is that you have that flexibility.

Spending three days at Alton Abbey has been very precious to me because I need perspective. I need to watch that the firm does not become iconic. It is not all I am! Sometimes I run on empty. I have not had a wellspring of God's love. It is so important to get life in balance. The Benedictine monastery is so important to me. The silence is wonderful. We all need to find a means of balance.

Healthy ambition is about being the best you can be. It is using power for the kingdom. It is not ruthlessly climbing over another person. It is so important to plug into the wider Christian community and allow different forms of prayer life. When difficult decisions have to be made, make them slowly. If possible, never make a decision the day it is first presented to you. Park it. Pray about it, and see what you think in the morning. God works through our unconscious mind as well as through our conscious mind. If, after reflection, the decision seems right, it is likely to be in accord with my values and the firm's values.

What is so evident in Stephen Bampfylde's story are:
- the importance of meditation and reflection
- the focus on high quality and integrity
- the recognition that you can easily be running on empty

Relevant questions arising from Stephen's thoughts might be:
- How do you best ensure top quality in what you do as a Christian leader in the secular world?
- Even though you are very busy, how do you create space for meditation and reflection?

- How do you pace yourself so that you are comfortable with the decisions you make?

Roger

My personal agenda is to be part of the transformation of the current world system into the kingdom. *Transformation* is a strong word, and it is best not to give it a timetable.

Two things that give me a buzz are being able to interpret for the Christian world what is going on in business and being able to encourage young Christians that it is fine to get involved in business. I have a suspicion that God is using Christians in business to be some sort of vanguard. Perhaps it is because we can experiment more freely, or maybe it is because, having been given a bit of encouragement, we're not going to sit quietly.

I feel uncomfortable about limiting Christianity to a good set of management principles, partly because that is far too tame. Also, business leaders have to achieve results. Jesus was playing a longer game; he was not seeking immediate results. I am not sure Jesus would have been a very good business leader in today's terms. One of his most distinctive features was that he left the freedom of choice to the people he was engaging with. He gave them the freedom to say no. In business, that would be a problem.

One time I was at the back of a church and picked up a book about St. Francis of Assisi. I realized there were bits of the Bible I was happy to apply at home and in church and other bits I was not so sure about when it came to my business life. It was a wake-up call that I was applying dual standards. Either the package was for real and it could be trusted, or it was not. So, for example, I made a conscious decision to try to apply humility not just at home but also at work. I don't blow my own trumpet at work anymore. I choose not to trust myself. I don't want to end up with a rampant ego.

I am conscious of the dangers of separating the Christian and the secular. I am aware that Christians in business can leave their Christian antennae behind. It is very easy to make a mistake when there is a tight judgment call, a mistake that is then shown to be dishonest. It is important to practice in the cricket net if you are going to play on the field. If you haven't practiced making good judgments in easy situations, you will make mistakes in tougher situations—perhaps because of the expectations of colleagues or customers. Observing people making tight judgment calls has taught me how dangerous it is to compromise one's Christian faith. It is clear that you need to have an almost instinctive understanding of the morality of your decisions. We must not absolve people from the responsibility to think for themselves.

Jesus was a leader with an extraordinary ability to assess each situation or person and hear from God and apply God's solution to that particular problem. What I see Jesus doing was often unbalanced. He could be very compassionate and then very assertive. Jesus was not a fan of balance. He did what was right in each situation. He was not lukewarm. He never chose the lesser of two evils.

Christians can be in danger of being manipulated. We have a tendency to trust people and not assume that others have agendas. It is also important to make sure we don't allow others to get away with assuming we are bigots just because we are Christians. We need to take the initiative to define what we want to be known for. We can choose to be known as people who have a high regard for others by doing practical things. If we do and say nothing, I'm afraid it will just be assumed that we represent what is worst about the church.

The experience of being at work is incredibly valuable. At home, people are nice to me! It is at work that I find out everything that is wrong with me. You learn who you are. This is where God sorts you out. I thank God that he treats me with grace.

I need to continuously find my identity only in Christ and not in my position or salary—it is essential that we hang on to that. We have to watch out for the danger of ego, false expectations, and unfulfilled dreams. Making a difference is important, but God has released me from the pressure of leaving a legacy. He is important; I am not.

It is crucial for Christians in their thirties and forties to have an excellent relationship with a mentor. I learned a lot from others about servant leadership and about giving people permission to make choices.

Some of the key themes that flow from Roger's story are:

- the importance of not leaving your "Christian antennae" behind
- the necessity of addressing ethical questions and not being browbeaten by the expectations of others
- the need to guard against being manipulated

Some questions to consider in light of Roger's reflections might be:

- Jesus could be both compassionate and assertive beyond the accepted norms of his day. What does that lack of "balance" mean for you?
- When a tight judgment call has to be made, have you practiced and prepared the way enough, or is there a danger that you might be compromised in certain situations?
- Do you have people around you who will mentor you, encourage you, and warn you if you are in danger of compromising your faith and your values?

SEE YOUR WORK AS A CHRISTIAN VOCATION

There is a danger that we view the concept of a "Christian vocation" as just about full-time Christian ministry or being involved in one of the caring professions. But we can live out a Christian vocation within a wide range of spheres. William Wilberforce talked of being "diligent in the business of life." Christian politicians, lawyers, engineers, technicians, IT specialists, and bankers are all making an important contribution to the economy and society in which they live. They are—or can be—contributing to making God's creation a better place by the way they carry out their responsibilities.

Figure 14 sets out the perspectives of a number of leaders about the way in which their work is a Christian vocation.

For individuals in full-time ministry, "Christian vocation" can be expressed simply as living out the ministry of Jesus. For those in the caring or teaching professions, the example of the leadership of Jesus is clear. For those contributing to effective government administration, making a difference in people's lives is an important motivation. In the commercial world, there can be a sense of vocation in enabling other people to fulfill their callings as well as in helping to create a fairer world.

Christian vocation can include the following elements:

- the activity itself
- the way the activity is carried out in terms of fairness and effectiveness
- the way issues are grappled with in the organization, thereby affecting its standards and values

Many professions and industries have within them Christians who are faithfully addressing intellectual and ethical issues that surface within that sector. In some cases there is an opportunity for open discourse about the relevance of Christian values to those working in that area.

One example of this is the way judges in England take forward their role. There is an annual service at Winchester Cathedral for judges in the

Figure 14

WORK AS CHRISTIAN VOCATION

"Christian vocation is about living out who I am and how God has made me. You make powerful choices about the kind of organization you want to work with. You then focus on improving the lot of people both inside and outside the organization."—*management consultant*

"My work has always been a vocation. The sense of doing something worthwhile is important. All human work has a purpose. The intrinsic act of working has a godliness in it. All our work and effort contributes. But as we work together there should be a sense of mystery and of being part of renewing God's creation together."—*HR director*

"Living your Christian vocation is about bringing an external perspective. It was disastrous when Christians persuaded people to believe in cultural norms such as apartheid. We are nowhere near as independent as we think. What are the assumptions that our grandchildren will criticize us for? Thirty percent of children are in single-parent homes. Why did we allow that to happen? There is a danger of endorsing nonideal behavior when there is economic pressure upon us."—*private sector leader*

"When you say that a particular career is your vocation, you may be hiding behind a veneer of Christianity. It is important to have, in our bipolar world, a proper integration between our faith and our work."—*international finance leader*

"Fulfilling my Christian vocation is about using the talent God has given me. My vocation is to try to create the right balance in the commercial world; it is providing an environment that releases the power in people. There is a danger in referring to people as 'staff'—as if they are something less than human. I have a passion to change the way we treat people in an organization. I believe that is God's vocation for me."—*HR director*

"Bringing a Christian vocation is about making a difference in people's lives. It is about how you treat people at work. It is not only the intellectual challenge but making the best use of God-given talent through stretching yourself."—*finance director*

"Christian vocation is about bringing fairness and standing up for the underdog. It is ensuring effective customer service. The danger is that we are trained to serve the system rather than lead and develop the system."—*private sector leader*

"The integration between faith and work is a priority in any sector, be it with students, in politics, or in banking. Raising finances to help with investment in developing countries is a profoundly Christian endeavor."—*senior international banker*

"Fulfilling our Christian vocation can include being part of a clear audit function in a finance organization in terms of watching disclosure, conflict of interest, and insider trading. Questions with ethical dimensions need to be addressed rigorously. It is not different in your private life, where key themes are service, transparency, and integrity."—*senior banker*

western half of the southwestern circuit. The Lord Chief Justice, Lord Igor Judge, spoke at the service in 2008 about the importance of judicial humility and judicial fortitude. Sir Igor looked at the relevance, for the judiciary, of Jesus washing his disciples' feet. Here are extracts from his sermon:

> It is a fundamental tenet of Christian faith—whether Protestant or Catholic—that Jesus was the son of God, and Omnipotent God. Yet here he is, washing feet. There is, first of all, the fact:

washing feet that had not been washed. More important, there is the symbolism: to wash his disciples' feet, their master must have lowered himself beneath them; he was crouching or on his knees before them.

The story reminds us of one judicial quality which never receives the attention it fully deserves. To be judges and magistrates needed by our own community we need many attributes. We need to be intelligent, knowledgeable about the law, but more importantly, perhaps, wise in the ways of the world, sensitive to others from different backgrounds than our own, fair and open-minded and balanced, independent in spirit, courageous to do what is right even when it will be unpopular—whether with politicians, the executive, or the media. But to all these ingredients I add one more: judicial humility. That is the message I derive from Jesus washing the disciples' feet.

Like everyone vested with power and authority—and we are indeed vested with power and authority—the power to lock up an individual and deprive him of his liberty, even for twenty-four hours, is a profound power. The most powerful judges in the world may indeed be the most powerful judges in the world, but they are and remain human beings, sitting on their own backsides, with the capacity for error, mistake, fallibility—that is part of our common humanity.

No trumpet blows for judicial modesty and humility, but they are nonetheless noble judicial qualities shared by the best of judges. I do not see humility as a rather feeble virtue. . . . For judges, there is no easy route to avoid error. We are all trying—all trying desperately hard, all the time—to avoid injustice: in the words of our oaths, to do "right" rather than "wrong."

It pains us all when mistakes are made. I am not talking about convictions quashed for technicalities. Every system of justice has its Kiszko moments. He was a truly innocent man convicted of murdering a small child, whose innocence was positively demonstrated many years later as a result of scientific developments. Collectively we shudder at such a desperately sad miscarriage of justice. But the route for judges and magistrates to avoid mistakes is for them to do nothing, to abjure their responsibilities, and to refuse to make a decision. That, however, is the coward's way out. It is no way out for us, or for the community we serve.

Day by day by day, judges up and down the country are making decisions which will have a dramatic effect on the lives of fellow human beings. Is this a prison case, or not? Will the offender learn more inside prison or outside it? What will he learn inside or outside? Should a child be removed from a parent? What will the effect on that child be? For the parent in the overwhelming majority of cases, it will be a disaster. And so on.

There is no way in which a judge can avoid making these decisions. They have to be made. Moreover, they have to be made when you know that they may be grossly criticized in the media—when you, as a judge, know that you must live with your judicial conscience and you must do right in the face of potential public criticism, which is deeply disturbing to your spouse and family.

Judicial humility, on its own, is not enough. And so, along with judicial humility, the administration of justice makes copious demands on another judicial quality: judicial fortitude. The entire story of the New Testament is the story of a man's fortitude—fortitude displayed when he knew full well the horrors that lay ahead for him, and when he would dearly have wished and, indeed, in one moment of human weakness sought to be free of the cup of anguish that lay ahead for him.*

And just as judicial humility does not for one moment imply judicial weakness, judicial fortitude does not carry with it vanity or arrogance. The passage of Jesus washing the disciples' feet reminds us that it is possible to be both humble and strong.

Sir Igor's sermon is an excellent example of an honest interrelationship between looking at the way Jesus acted and decisions that a particular profession needs to make. Valuable questions to ask include:

- This sermon is about judicial humility and fortitude. To what extent do the same principles apply in other areas of work?
- What is the right balance between humility and fortitude?
- How might the story of Jesus washing the disciples' feet be relevant in your area of work?

SEE TURBULENCE AS AN OPPORTUNITY

The natural reaction when we see turbulence around us is to keep our distance and protect ourselves. During times of turbulence, we can feel vulnerable both professionally and personally. We think that we might lose our job or our reputation. Can we see turbulence as an opportunity rather than a threat?

The people of Israel survived turbulent times. They held on to their central belief in God as the Lord Almighty. There was a stability about God that was not going to be undermined, whatever the turbulence. When we enter a period of turbulence, perhaps it is a time to do the following:

- Reflect on the way the Old Testament characters lived through turbulence.

- Recall words of the Psalms or Proverbs that give us a sense of living in God's created order, where there is a sense of purpose even through turbulence. Take, for example, the words of Psalm 25:4–6: "Show me your ways, LORD, teach me your paths. Guide me in your truth and teach me, for you are God my Savior, and my hope is in you all day long. Remember, LORD, your great mercy and love, for they are from of old."
- Remember how you have lived through turbulence effectively before.
- Try to see what good can come out of this particular turbulent situation.
- Recognize that your whole life does not depend on successfully coping with this spate of turbulence.
- Accept that sometimes the passage of events goes in your favor, and sometimes it doesn't.

A lesson from the Old Testament is that turbulence can be the norm rather than the exception. Our lives may run in phases, with varying degrees of turbulence. But when they do turn upside down, perhaps it is a matter of saying, "Hallelujah anyway!" As Christians, we may be better able to cope with turbulence because of the centrality of our faith through all we think and do. When you feel turbulence, let Jesus' words of comfort and grace help lift you to a better place.

TIME TO THINK, REFLECT, AND PRAY

Creating space to think, reflect, and pray can be a positive experience both in terms of creating the space and in using the opportunities that are then presented to us. In his book *Do Nothing to Change Your Life*, Bishop Stephen Cottrell recounts his experience of using unexpected moments to good effect while he was stranded at the Dublin airport for five hours.

There was a restless impatience within me. I was cross with myself for not getting the time right. I was cross with the situation: so much time being wasted. The minutes ticked by with aching slowness. The hours before me were an unwanted eternity. But then, imperceptibly, a calm came over me. The next four hours did not have to be a problem. They did not have to be a waste. Rather, they could be a gift. And as this thought settled in my mind I found I was able to just sit down and be still, and find contentment without having to be busy. I could relax and just be.[1]

After the restlessness waned, Bishop Stephen got a notebook and began to play with ideas, and slowly a poem was born. In moments of "idleness," something creative was born. He wrote, "When I speak about what happens when we do nothing I am not in any way wanting to exalt laziness. Rather, I want to celebrate what happens when we dare to stop and reconnect with a hiddenness inside ourselves where rest and play issue forth in all sorts of wild, unexpected and creative ways."[2]

Moments of idleness can provide some of the most precious moments, as out of our emptiness new ideas or creativity can flow when we combine different aspects of our thinking and understanding in a powerful way.

Sometimes we find it very difficult to take time to think, reflect, and pray. We are driven by activity and find it very difficult to stop. Figure 15 is a comparison between Psalm 23 and "Not Psalm 23," in which the writer summarizes the way we often live our lives whereby "deadlines and my need for approval, they drive me." The result can be that "surely fatigue and time pressure shall follow me all the days, hours and minutes of my life. And I will dwell in the bonds of frustration forever."

---

1.   From the introduction to Stephen Cottrell, *Do Nothing to Change Your Life: Discovering What Happens When You Stop* (New York: Seabury Books, 2008).
2.   Ibid.

Figure 15

RECOGNIZING WHAT WE ARE DRIVEN BY	
Psalm 23	"Not Psalm 23"
The LORD is my shepherd, I lack nothing. He makes me lie down in green pastures, he leads me beside quiet waters, he refreshes my soul. He guides me along the right paths for his name's sake. Even though I walk through the darkest valley, I will fear no evil, for you are with me; your rod and your staff, they comfort me. You prepare a table before me in the presence of my enemies. You anoint my head with oil; my cup overflows. Surely your goodness and love will follow me all the days of my life, and I will dwell in the house of the LORD forever.	The clock is my dictator, I shall not rest. It maketh me lie down only when exhausted. It leads me to deep depression, it hounds my soul. It leads me in circles of frenzy for activity's sake. Even though I run frantically from task to task, I will never get it all done. For my "ideal" is with me. Deadlines and my need for approval, they drive me. They demand performance from me, beyond the limits of my schedule. They anoint my head with migraines, my in-tray overfloweth. Surely fatigue and time pressure shall follow me all the days, hours and minutes of my life. And I will dwell in the bonds of frustration forever. Written by Marcia K. Hornok Used by permission.

The best way of creating space to think, reflect, and pray will vary from one person to another. The key thing is to ask the right questions of yourself or get other people to ask you those questions.

- When do you think most clearly: for example, early in the morning, traveling to work, doing physical exercise on the weekend, while reflecting with good friends?
- Do you reflect most effectively in the privacy of your own thinking or in conversation with those you trust?
- How does prayer best work for you: for example, in a structured way in a private space, or as you are traveling to or from work and you know that you will not be disturbed?

Key questions leading to your next steps might be:
- When do you best think, reflect, and pray?
- What routines do you want to develop further to help you do this?
- How will you hold yourself accountable?
- Who can you ask to encourage you and to share these aspects of your life journey with you?

THINK AHEAD ABOUT TIME AND ENERGY

Our lives are finite. The focus and preoccupation of one day may be absolutely right, but they might need to be different in a month's or a year's time. So often we feel a strong sense of doing the right thing now and don't always recognize that this will change over time. Recognizing that the whole of the Old Testament is about a sense of journey can help reinforce the perspective that what we are doing now might be entirely right, but that the sense of movement and journey may be taking us to a different place.

Our lives may have a sequence of phases. We may be spending a lot of time with the young people in our lives now, but when they have "left the nest," they will want to be much more selective about the time they spend with us. Our working lives will move from phase to phase, eventually with the potential shock of retirement.

There is the need both to be fully present in what we are doing now and to be responsible to think through the future. Developing skills now for use in the future is a responsible use of our time and talents. Recognizing that we will not always be fit to do the activities we want is being realistic.

Key questions to ask might be:
- What might be your next stage in terms of Christian service?
- What gifts has God given you that it would be good to develop further?

- What can be done only now—and to which you therefore need to bring a sense of urgency?

BE HONEST ABOUT AMBITION

What is proper ambition? Is it about modesty and making sure that your ambition doesn't interfere with more "godly" priorities? Is ambition good, or does it involves "selling our soul to Caesar"?

Ambition properly understood and directed can be a great influence for good. Ambition to make a difference for the benefit of individuals or communities is a powerful force for good, as many teachers or members of the caring professions will testify. But is ambition acceptable for those in government, finance, or business? When does ambition to make a difference become ambition for influence or financial returns? These elements are sometimes intertwined; we often live with inconsistencies in our own preferences and behaviors.

The starting point is to be honest about our ambition and ask ourselves questions like:

- Where does my ambition come from? Is it related to serving me or serving others?
- Is my ambition enabling or destructive of others?
- Is my ambition evolving in the light of experience and new insights, or is it stuck in earlier misconceptions?
- How comfortable would I be talking through my ambitions with the risen Christ?

Ambition in and of itself is not a bad thing. The question is what the ambition is for and how it impacts others. There may well be different phases of life where ambition moves from one priority to another. Perhaps the biggest risk is being fixated on one type of ambition and not cross-checking the extent to which it is compatible with your Christian values and understanding. Allowing ourselves to look anew at our ambitions on a periodic basis is healthy.

FIND YOUR FUTURE: THE SECOND TIME AROUND

Finding your future is what eighteen- to twenty-two-year-olds are supposed to do. For the rest of us, finding our future was something we tried to do once; but, strangely, we seem to have to do it again and again and again! As adults, we assume we should have found our future and that we should be living it. What if we are bored, frustrated, or downhearted? Do we have to stand still? Sometimes it feels as if our only option is to stay where we are and paper over the cracks. You've made your bed; now lie in it!

We don't want to settle for second best. We don't want to be continually frustrated or feel a sense of failure. Maybe a major event has happened that has forced us to reexamine our priorities. Perhaps there has been a bereavement, job change, loss of a job, or the children have left home. We are ready to reassess our lives. Well, at least some of the time we feel this way!

Starting Points

Where do we begin? I explore many potential starting points in my book *Finding Your Future: The Second Time Around*. The possibilities include:

- seeing **failure** as a gift
- living with your **fears**
- coping with your **frustrations**
- learning from your own **fortitude**

Working through failures, acknowledging and understanding our fears, being honest about our frustrations, and embedding the learning from moments of fortitude can provide a basis from which to move forward.

Sometimes failure can be a gift. When one door closes, however hard it bangs, there can be other doors to press. Sometimes our failures prompt a complete change in direction. We are focused on one set of goals and aspirations, and the shock of our failure sends us in a different direction. Sometimes the seed has to die before there can be new birth (see John 12:24). If there is a past failure that still rankles, can we "slay that dragon" and move on and put it behind us?

Fear of the future can gnaw inside us like a cancer. It can grow and eat away our hope and joy. But fear can be greatly overrated; most of our worst fears never come to pass. As we look to the future, it may be that we need to understand our fears better, get them in proportion, and live through the fear of change. In the words of the apostle John, "Perfect love drives out fear" (1 John 4:18)—hence the value of faith, family, friends, and community when the future is uncertain.

Taking Stock

There are moments when standing back is important in order to reflect on the wider influences upon you. Important factors include:

- the influence of your **family** background and current **family** situation
- the importance of your **friends**
- constraints and options about **finances**
- the **fundamentals** that are most important to you

These elements can provide a framework for taking stock about where we have come from and what is important to us for the future.

Being clear about the fundamentals that matter most can provide the clarity that enables us to move on. What are your most fundamental beliefs about yourself and your world? What is more important to you than anything else? How do you want to be remembered? What are the values that you consider most important and that you are determined to live by?

Our family backgrounds influence our values, behaviors, beliefs, aspirations, and fears. Our cultural backgrounds give us a framework for living, but our own experiences will often lead to contradictions in ourselves. Taking stock gives us a wonderful opportunity to look again at our values, what we draw from our family and cultural background, and what strengths we want to build on for the future.

Looking Forward

Looking forward is where the hard work begins, where boldness in our thinking and action becomes important. There may be very different strands in regard to looking forward, such as:

- the importance of **forgiveness**, especially of ourselves
- following our **fascinations**
- being clear about the degree of **freedom** we have and how we want to use it
- the use of **fasting** and self-denial as an aid

Sometimes it is only when forgiveness takes root that we can begin to look forward with untarnished sight. Allowing ourselves to follow our fascinations can take us out of ourselves and into a new perspective. Realism about the degree of freedom we do or do not have is essential. Fasting or self-denial may be one element of preparing for our next steps.

Sometimes forgiveness of others may be reasonably straightforward: for example, when one of the children in your life keeps letting himself or herself and you down or when a colleague has made a mistake and is determined to learn from it. Forgiveness may not be as easy when a colleague manipulates what you say in a damaging way or a friend abuses your trust.

Finding our future will often involve coming to terms with situations or relationships where there is resentment. Sometimes there will be an oscillation between resentment and forgiveness. But forgiveness can be a cathartic next step in moving on. Only when you have forgiven somebody whom you feel has wronged you can the anger be dispersed. Remembering moments when we have been forgiven can be an important reminder of our humanity. As I suggested earlier, if forgiving others is tough, forgiving ourselves can be in another league altogether!

The theme of fasting is based on understanding our addictions and what is holding us back. It means being clear about what we are dependent upon and then occasionally stepping back. Along with food, of course, we might be addicted to electronic communications or cars or new clothes.

Moving On

Moving on, if it is going to be permanent, is likely to include:
- clear **foresight**, looking five years ahead
- a **focus** on key priorities
- a strong sense of **fun** and seeing the lighter side
- **fulfillment** that fully embraces what is important to us

Sometimes moving on will involve spontaneous decisions, but more often significant next steps will result from careful thought. Trying to look ahead with foresight can provide a framework for our decisions. Being focused can help us discriminate between important priorities and those that are less important. A sense of fun is an essential prerequisite for being energized as we move forward. Looking for fulfillment that is consistent with our personal beliefs and values is necessary for our own peace of mind. Moving on is about making decisions that stick while still being able to laugh at ourselves and our foibles.

As you look ahead, are you sometimes too serious for your own good? Is the absence of joy an indicator that you need to monitor? Sometimes the heaviness of life is unavoidable. But do you also have a link to fun and relaxation? Can you seek out a means of giving yourself and others a lift?

Even when life seems really tough and decisions seem especially difficult, it is helpful to:
- look for the absurd in any situation
- try to smile, and observe what other people do as a result
- bring a lighter touch in order to gently steer discussions
- relive your most joyful moments before making difficult decisions
- make relaxation and a sense of fun a high priority as one component of life

Fulfillment is not about winning every battle. Many day-to-day tasks may seem like drudgery. Creating long-term fulfillment is about:
- allowing ourselves to be renewed each time we feel hurt or

knocked down

- allowing hope to spring eternal by seeing each incident as one step on our pathway rather than an end in itself
- allowing ourselves to spend enough time in our defining moments to embrace and enjoy them
- allowing ourselves to continue to grow in our emotional and spiritual understanding

Living Hopefully

Finding your future is not about reckless acts that are not rooted in realism. First it is about being very clear concerning the constraints upon you and your obligations to others. Then it is about being bold and setting off on the next step of your life's journey, determined to make a difference in your chosen sphere.

Never give up on the hope of transformation. We have the capacity for new birth, new ideas, new experiences, and discovering new qualities in ourselves. If we believe that renewal is possible, both in our lives and in the lives of others, we can hold together practical optimism and realism. In the words of Henry Wadsworth Longfellow,

> Let us, then, be up and doing
> With a heart for any fate;
> Still achieving, still pursuing,
> Learn to labor, and to wait.

ALLOW YOURSELF TO BE SURPRISED

We like to plan and prepare for our next steps. We may be immersed in a working environment where there is clarity about the vision and the priorities. We may have clear objectives and a personal development plan. Planning for the future effectively is exercising responsibility well. But how do we respond to surprises?

When I left my career in government to move into executive coaching, I had a clear plan related to coaching. What took me by surprise was the opportunity to write. In the last six years I have had the opportunity to write ten books on either leadership or leadership and spirituality. Though I had written many ministerial speeches and government publications, I had never envisioned the possibility of writing for a wider audience. Hence my surprise and delight when the opportunity came.

However much we plan and think ahead, there will be surprises. Some of them, resulting from economic turbulence or health or other personal circumstances, will be unwelcome and unpleasant. We will embrace other surprises, which lift us and give us joy, as gifts from God.

Questions to ask yourself might be:
- Are you ready to be pleasantly surprised in your daily life?
- Are you open-minded enough to accept that God may well be leading you in new and different directions?

BE A PIONEER

Alan Smith is the recently appointed bishop of St. Albans. In an interview with him, he spoke to me about the prophetic and pioneering role of the Christian leader. He pointed out how Christians over the centuries have pioneered different enterprises—for example, in education, health, and social services. Observing that Christian missionaries and traders were the great adventurers of the past, Alan challenges the Christian in the secular world today to be a pioneer.

What pioneering role might you take forward? It could be trying to change the values of your organization or building a greater awareness of green or ethical issues or the way different members of the organization are treated. A pioneering role might mean leaving your current role and taking action in a different direction. It might require pushing the boundaries of your abilities so that you develop skills that have been dormant till now.

An investment banker with a vision of contributing to the development of entrepreneurship in Africa recently came to see me. He admitted that this was a rather vague aspiration, but he was determined to test the boundaries and see what might be possible. I tried to encourage him, though not in a way that would build up false hopes. We talked about how he could focus his energies over the next twelve months to see what contacts he could make. We prayed together. My contribution was to invite him to be focused within a particular time period in which he would bring energy, vision, and prayerfulness—and allow himself to be open to the fact that the venture might succeed or it might not. Whatever the outcome, he was striving to serve God and to be both passionate and practical at the same time.

Key questions to ask yourself might be:
- Is there a pioneering element within you?
- If you were to "pioneer" something, what would it be?
- Who might support you in this process, giving you encouragement as well as keeping you realistic?
- What practical next steps would be appropriate to take?

BE SUPPORTED BY OTHERS

To be strong is to be independent, right? We like to feel that we are not dependent on others. But we all know how much impact an encouraging word from a trusted friend or colleague can have.

I was a member of a board that was particularly successful because the individual members were committed to each other's success. There was an honest process of feedback at the end of meetings. We knew that the board's impact was greater than the sum of its parts. We had a high degree of confidence in each other, which meant that we were willing to be supported by our colleagues.

Being supported by others might include our family, friends, work colleagues, and a mentor or coach. Allowing ourselves to be supported by others is not a sign of weakness; it is a recognition of our humanity. Jesus sent out his disciples in pairs because he knew the importance of mutual support. Paul took a companion with him on his missionary travels, be it Barnabas or Silas.

As you share with those you trust, where does prayer fit in? When I am coaching a Christian, sometimes we conclude our time together with prayer. It feels, then, that there are three rather than two parties engaged in working out the right next steps. It is a powerful experience to work through different options with a Christian and then to stand back and, through reflective prayer, seek clarity of thinking so that emotional distortions are minimized and God's purposes are allowed to fall into place.

There are so many illustrations of individuals being supported well by others. As an illustration, Thomas has held senior roles in the private and public sectors. He has encouraged people to know what they stand for and emphasizes the mantra of knowing, being, and doing. He acknowledges the nourishment that comes from the Gospel reading every Sunday, as the lesson always has elements in it that are relevant for leadership. He knows that faith gives us serenity. It is about letting Christ shine through in the way we make decisions; it is calmly living in the Spirit.

Thomas admits to being driven and a bit of a perfectionist. Being cared for by others is important to him. Others in the church have "scooped him up" in times of personal sadness. He appreciates the mutual support of friends in his Christian community—for instance, the value of a breakfast together to strengthen him for the day or for the weekend. Friendships have been particularly important to him in coping with a very demanding job.

Key questions to ask in regard to being supported by others might include:

- Who in the past has provided the best type of feedback and enabled you to grow effectively as a leader?
- Who do you naturally go to now when you want to talk through an issue? When you are just looking for comfort? When you are ready to be stretched in your thinking?

CONTRIBUTE TO YOUR LOCAL CHRISTIAN COMMUNITY

Just as a Christian leader brings a strong awareness of the life and work of Jesus into his or her work in the secular world, so a Christian who has had experience in the business or administrative world has a wealth of knowledge and understanding to bring to leadership within Christian organizations. I have developed the following illustrative insights from my discussions with a wide range of different people.

John has had a number of leadership roles. He believes that what a Christian with experience of the secular world can bring to Christian organizations is a clarity of objectives. It is about cutting out extraneous noise. It is providing a constant reminder and bridge between sacred and secular and bringing a perspective that is wider than the local church. John believes that we need to remind church leaders that they are there to serve others and not the other way around. His vision is enabling church leaders to enable Christians to fulfill their work in the world; it is very important to have a holistic vision and not be constrained by a purely local interpretation.

A former university administrator spoke of bringing the experience of the university world into the church. Sometimes this means bringing a dose of reality and sometimes a lightness of touch. He commented that there is a danger of getting things out of perspective in a church context and not having clarity about relative levels of importance.

A finance director in a large organization recounted withdrawing from being part of the church leadership committee before he got too irritable. He observed that moving from the discipline of a secular organization to working in a voluntary organization can be challenging. A problem is that there is not enough time to do strategic thinking when there are a lot of detailed issues and church politics to work through.

The amount of time that Christian leaders in the secular world can give to leadership roles in the church world will vary as they progress through their careers. A key factor will be the amount of time available for family, which will fluctuate depending on the ages of children and the health of aging parents. The right equilibrium will be different at different stages of life. But bringing an independent perspective to leadership of Christian organizations can have a very powerful impact, providing clarity and a sense of practical reality when those directly involved cannot see beyond the immediate issues.

Some will resonate with Henry, a senior leader in a large organization, for whom the local church community is very important. He has long since given up being a member of the governing body of the church. He does not go to church to be in charge; his role is to be a servant. He works with the disadvantaged. Henry says that his involvement with the community keeps him sane. He did a number of years of youth work, which helped him to see things from other people's perspective. His nourishment at church comes from the sacrament of Holy Communion. It is so special to him because it is the fundamental remembrance of a sacrificial life. It is a celebration of God's love, as a consequence, and everyone is doing the same thing irrespective of who they are as they come up to receive Communion.

On weekends, Henry helps someone who is homebound get out of the house. On Sundays, when he goes to church, he looks after somebody who is disabled. What nourishes him is the recognition of close friends who are traveling on the same journey of faith.

Henry's Christian faith and involvement have taught him to be relaxed in any circumstance. What is important to him is serving others and not asserting his own rights, treating people as individuals rather than labeling them as a group, not ignoring people in the street. While Henry is concerned that sermons do not often relate to his experience, he is very clear that being a Christian sustains him and provides an important resource for him. Being part of a church means spending time supporting each other and encouraging each other to go out of their way to live sacrificial lives. What matters is building a community of redemption, not worrying too much about theology or being overly prescriptive about particular theological truths. While Henry recognizes that hard messages often have to be given and difficult decisions often have to be made, being concerned about people as individuals is at the center of both his leadership within the secular world and his involvement within the local church.

Key questions to ask might be:

- What contribution do you currently make within your local church or wider community?
- What is the most appropriate value-added contribution that you could make?
- Is there a role from which you should withdraw in order to let others have an opportunity to make a difference?

LIVE LIFE TO THE FULL

As part of the Sermon on the Mount, Jesus said, "Therefore I tell you, do not worry about your life, what you will eat or drink; or about your body, what you will wear. Is not life more important than food, and the body more important than clothes? Look at the birds of the air; they do not sow or reap or store away in barns, and yet your heavenly Father feeds them. Are you not much more valuable than they? Can any one of you by worrying add a single hour to your life?" (Matthew 6:25–27).

Reflecting on these verses, Tom Wright, in his commentary *Matthew for Everyone*, wrote:

> When Jesus told his followers not to worry about tomorrow, we must assume that he led them by example. He wasn't always looking ahead anxiously, making the present moment count only because of what might come next. No: he seems to have had the skill of living totally in the present, giving attention totally to the present task, celebrating the goodness

of God here and now. If that's not a recipe for happiness, I don't know what is.

And he wanted his followers to do the same. When he urged them to make God their priority it's important to realize which God he's talking about. He's not talking about a god who is distant from the world, who doesn't care about beauty and life and food and clothes. He's talking about the Creator himself, who has filled the world with wonderful and mysterious things, full of beauty and energy and excitement, and who wants his human creatures above all to trust him and love him and receive their own beauty, energy and excitement from him."[3]

Wright stresses that living totally without worry sounds, to many people, as impossible as living totally without breathing. Some people are so hooked on worry that if they don't have anything to worry about they worry that they have forgotten something![4]

Being renewed is about keeping life in proportion. It is about both working hard and accepting that it is right to live in the moment. Jesus wasn't saying that we shouldn't plant seeds and reap harvests or that we shouldn't work at weaving and spinning to make clothes. Rather, we should do these things with joy, because our God, our Father, is the Creator of all and wants to feed and clothe us.

We can so easily allow worry to get a grip on us and limit our ability to live in the moment and to be fully absorbed with the people and the context of our lives. How easily we let worry about tomorrow get in the way so that we do not live life to the full—and bring encouragement to others as a conduit of God's love.

---

3.   Tom Wright, *Matthew for Everyone: Part 1: Chapters 1–15* (London: SPCK Publishing, 2002), 66.
4.   Ibid.

Key questions to ask might be:

- When does worry get in the way in your life? How can that be limited?
- How can you be fully absorbed in the moment more effectively?
- How can you be more of a conduit of God's love and purposes each day at work?

CONCLUSION

In this section we have looked at being renewed. We have reflected on allowing ourselves to learn from others; to see our work as a Christian vocation; to see turbulence as an opportunity, to take time to think, reflect, and pray; to be honest about ambition; to look ahead to the future, allowing ourselves to be surprised; to be a pioneer, to be supported by others; to contribute to our local Christian community; and to live life to the full.

Some final reflections:

- Who are you continuing to learn from?
- In what ways could you see your current work even more clearly as a Christian vocation?
- How could you allow yourself more time to think, reflect, and pray?
- What opportunities can you take to specifically consider your future, including ways that God might want to surprise you?
- In what new ways could you be supported by others?
- How might you contribute in a more focused way to your local Christian community?
- In what respects can you live life to the full as a Christian without being tainted by worry?

NEXT STEPS

We can so often feel, as the hymn writer put it, like "frail children of dust." We can be overwhelmed by the pressures of life, the manipulation of others, our own misfortunes or the misfortunes of others, the inequities that surround us, or our own failings. Rather than being a bold Christian in the secular world, we want to hide away and feel sorry for ourselves.

The example of Jesus is so helpful. He was willing to break the mold. He made his own decisions; he challenged the authorities; he built a team of disciples from a selection of seemingly random individuals. He told stories and made people think in fresh ways. He caused both excitement and irritation. He was engaged and active, as well as quiet and prayerful. He lived firmly within the world, but he was certainly not dominated by the world (see John 17:14–16).

Christian leaders in the secular world have a foot in both camps. We need to understand the secular world in which we operate, but we also bring insights from our Christian faith and understanding. We are able to follow the example of Jesus, who was completely engaged in the affairs of the day and yet also brought a detached objectivity. When we look through the eyes of Jesus, we see clarity of purpose together with a wealth of compassion. There was the hard edge of intent combined with a gentle ability to be with people in whatever their circumstances.

Being a Christian leader in the global world is not about embracing whatever the current socially accepted norms happen to be. Instead, it is about bringing a strong sense of the life of Christ and the fruit of the Spirit so that transformation can take place and the workplace can be redeemed rather than damned. Having a profound Christian influence in the secular world is not about clichés or sermons. It is about living and exemplifying faith, hope, and love.

My hope is that this book has helped you recognize the value of being rooted in Jesus as Lord, has kindled your desire to be radical in following Jesus the Redeemer, and has encouraged you to be reflective and renewed through engagement with Jesus the Savior and Teacher.

In terms of next steps, for some it will mean working through different sections of the book and the questions at the end of each subsection. For others it may mean writing an action plan. For others it will mean standing back and seeing which points resonate most—letting your subconscious do the thinking and letting the Holy Spirit speak to your heart and mind. Maybe you need to be more rooted or radical or reflective or renewed. Be open to personal growth in faith, confidence, and understanding. Be upheld by God's love as you quietly reflect on the calling you have to be a Christian leader in the global world and to be diligent in the business of life.

SELECTED
BIBLIOGRAPHY

Anand, N., ed. *Change: How to Adapt and Transform the Business.* Norwich, UK: Format, 2004.

Bakke, Dennis W. *Joy at Work: A Revolutionary Approach to Fun on the Job.* Seattle: PVG, 2005.

Bibb, Sally, and Jeremy Kourdi. *Trust Matters: For Organisational and Personal Success.* Basingstoke, UK: Palgrave Macmillan, 2004.

Buckingham, Marcus, and Donald Clifton. *Now, Discover Your Strengths.* New York: Pocket Books, 2004.

Buford, Bob. *Stuck in Halftime.* Grand Rapids: Zondervan, 2001.

Collins, Jim. *Good to Great.* London: Random House, 2001.

Costa, Ken. *God at Work: Living Every Day with Purpose.* London: Continuum, 2007.

Cottrell, Stephen. *Do Nothing to Change Your Life: Discovering What Happens When You Stop.* New York: Seabury Books, 2008.

Covey, Stephen R. *The Seven Habits of Highly Effective People.* New York: Simon & Schuster, 1989.

CPAS. *Growing Leaders.* Warwick, UK: CPAS, 2006.

Dow, Graham. *A Christian Understanding of Daily Work.* Cambridge: Grove, 1996.

France, R. T., *Matthew.* Leicester, UK: Inter-Varsity, 1985.

Green, Rodney. *90,000 Hours: Managing the World of Work,* Bletchley, UK: Scripture Union, 2002.

Hammond, John S., Ralph L. Keeney, and Howard Raiffa. *Smart Choices: A Practical Guide to Making Better Life Decisions.* New York: Broadway Books, 1999.

Hill, Alexander. *Christian Ethics for the Marketplace.* Downers Grove, IL: InterVarsity, 2008.

Hirst, Judy. *Struggling to Be Holy.* London: Darton, Longman and Todd, 2006.

Hybels, Bill. *Courageous Leadership.* Grand Rapids: Zondervan, 2002.

Lawrence, James. *Growing Leaders: Reflections on Leadership, Life and Jesus.* Abingdon, UK: Bible Reading Fellowship, 2004.

Lewis, C. S. *Mere Christianity.* London: Fount, 1997.

Nouwen, Henri. *Bread for the Journey.* London: Darton, Longman and Todd, 1996.

_____. *In the Name of Jesus: Reflections on Christian Leadership.* New York: Crossroad, 1989.

Packer, J. I., and Carolyn Nystrom. *Guard Us, Guide Us: Divine Leading in Life's Decisions.* Grand Rapids: Baker, 2008.

Shaw, Peter. *Business Coaching: Achieving Practical Results through Effective Engagement* (coauthored with Robin Linnecar). Chichester, UK: Capstone, 2007.

_____. *Deciding Well: A Christian Perspective on Making Decisions as a Leader.* Vancouver: Regent College Publishing, 2009.

_____. *Making Difficult Decisions: How to Be Decisive and Get the Business Done.* Chichester, UK: Capstone, 2008.

_____. *Mirroring Jesus as Leader.* Cambridge: Grove, 2004.

_____. *Raise Your Game: How to Succeed at Work.* Chichester, UK: Capstone, 2009.

Smith, Gordon T. *The Voice of Jesus: Discernment, Prayer and the Witness of the Spirit.* Downers Grove, IL: InterVarsity, 2003.

Waltke, Bruce K. *Finding the Will of God: A Pagan Notion?* Grand Rapids: Eerdmans; Vancouver: Regent College Publishing, 2002.

Watson, Andrew. *The Fourfold Leadership of Jesus.* Abingdon, UK: Barnabas, 2008.

Wright, Tom. *Matthew for Everyone: Part 1: Chapters 1-15.* London: SPCK Publishing, 2002.

Wright, Walter. *Relational Leadership.* 2nd ed. Colorado Springs: Authentic, 2009.